Lessing's "Ugly Ditch":
A Study of Theology and History

Lessing's "Ugly Ditch": A Study Of Theology And History

Gordon E. Michalson, Jr.

The Pennsylvania State University Press
University Park and London

To the Memory of Carl Michalson
1915–1965

Library of Congress Cataloging in Publication Data

Michalson, Gordon E., 1948–
Lessing's "ugly ditch."

Includes bibliography and index.
1. History (Theology)—History of doctrines.
2. Lessing, Gotthold Ephraim, 1729–1787.   3. Protestant
churches—Doctrines—History—20th century.   I. Title.
BR115.H5M485   1985   231.7'6   84–42991
ISBN 0–271–00385–5

Contents

Preface

Karl Barth once complained that modern theological discussion is too much like a newspaper photograph taken during a frenzied moment at a soccer match. The stop-action shot shows players from both sides lunging chaotically, faces contorted, arms outstretched, legs askew. The curious feature of the photograph, Barth pointed out, is that, for all the action, the ball is nowhere in sight.

More than most, Barth thought he knew what to keep in sight and how to do it. My ambition in this book is considerably less: I aim mainly to draw attention to a set of confusions and misunderstandings bearing on the perennial problem of Christian faith's relation to history. These confusions arise largely because of the ways in which G.E. Lessing's famous image of the "ugly ditch" between historical truth and religious truth has been appropriated during the past two centuries of Protestant thought. Indeed, in large measure this book is intended to separate out and clarify the several different things that Lessing himself may have meant by the "ugly ditch."

I offer no grand historical account of precisely how and why the image of the ditch has confused or—better still—immobilized us. Certainly I have my hunches, hunches informed by Wittgenstein's insight that we "predicate of the thing what lies in the method of representing it."[1] I mainly intend, however, to say what I trust are some clear words about a very familiar topic, weaving my narrative together through accounts of well-known figures such as Lessing himself, Kierkegaard, Troeltsch, and Bultmann. I hope to show how the very familiarity of my topic has both numbed us to the nuances of Lessing's image and structured the modern debate over faith and history in ways that guarantee impasse and frustration. That Christian faith stands in *some* relation to history is undeniable. I simply want to cast doubt on the notion that we have to discuss this relation in the terms dictated by two centuries' worth of unrefined refer-

[1]Ludwig Wittgenstein, *Philosophical Investigations*, trans. G.E.M. Anscombe (New York: Macmillan, 1958), sect. 104, p. 46.

ences to Lessing's "ugly ditch," while simultaneously clarifying what the so-called ditch itself is all about.

Consequently, although I speak of this work in the introduction as primarily an exercise in philosophical untangling, it is not too far-fetched to think of it as well as a diagnosis of a theological illness. And, in due course, the reader who grasps the point of my diagnosis may be eager for some theological therapy. Such a reader will be disappointed, for I offer none. This is mainly because to offer therapy would in fact be to undermine my entire project, since I am not arguing that proposed treatments of theological diseases caused by the ditch have hitherto been ineffective, but that the very employment of ditch imagery in the discussion of faith and history is itself the chief symptom of the disease. The deeper issue, really, is not even that we suffer the disease of confusion, but that we are *unaware* that we suffer from it. In a situation such as this, something closer to conversion than to therapy is probably called for. At any rate, a true "cure" here would not consist of a "solution" to "the problem of faith and history," but an emerging sense of ironic detachment toward the way in which we have traditionally conceptualized the problem.

Theologically speaking, the closest thing to a truly constructive standpoint lurking in these pages lurks only in the form of a subplot. Especially in the later chapters, it may gradually dawn on the reader that I am associating the pernicious influence of ditch imagery with the entire process of the "academicizing" of Protestant theology since Schleiermacher. If I am right in making this connection, then the wheel-spinning that goes on in the mud of Lessing's ditch is intimately connected with the increasingly technical and arcane character of modern Protestant theology, forged in an idiom that makes problems of Christian faith appear to be fundamentally "intellectual" and "technical" in character—the stuff of university life, calling for sophisticated new conceptual and "methodological" approaches that will no doubt spawn new discussion sections at professional meetings.

Moreover—and here I suppose I *am* with Barth, insofar as I grasp what that could possibly mean—my argument throughout this book concerning too much talk about the wrong topic invariably contains hints of what I think the right topic is. The wrong topic, as the reader will quickly learn, is historical criticism and the procedures of historical research as they relate to Christian faith. The right topic, by contrast, is historical revelation. In other words, the wrong topic is wrong partly because it reflects the concerns of the secular, academic sensibility, while the right topic is right because it is what animates and sustains the worshipping community. Serious questions of intelligibility naturally and appropriately arise in connection with any talk about historical revelation. These questions, however, become mesmerizing only if, with Schleiermacher, we commit the fatal error of permitting the cultured despisers to define the theological agenda. When that happens, as it seems to have happened in the last two centuries, we get what we perhaps deserve: theologians who *are* the cultured despisers.

This book has been percolating for quite some time and has gone through a number of phases. Portions of the research connected with this project have previously appeared in article form: "Lessing, Kierkegaard, and the 'Ugly Ditch': A Reexamination," *Journal of Religion* 59 (1979); and "Theology, Historical Knowledge, and the Contingency-Necessity Distinction," *International Journal for Philosophy of Religion* 14 (1983). As is typically the case with these things, the successful completion of the entire project occurred neither by accident nor solely through the energies of the author. Both the National Endowment for the Humanities and Oberlin College have been generous with grant money, the former through a Summer Stipend and a Fellowship for College Teachers, the latter through an H.H. Powers Travel Grant. Oberlin has been generous as well with both leave time and moral support, and I am deeply grateful to Robert Longsworth, former dean of the Oberlin faculty, to Provost Sam Carrier, and to some very special denizens—past and present—of the Oberlin community: Grover Zinn, Keith Boone, Lyn Boone, Susan Kane, Larry Shinn, Gil Meilaender, Clyde Holbrook, and Cynthia Scherr.

The bulk of the original manuscript was written while I enjoyed the 1980–81 academic year as a visiting fellow in Princeton University's Department of Religion. I am grateful to the entire department for its warm collegiality, and especially to Malcolm Diamond and Jeffrey Stout, who took time to read and comment upon emerging chapters and to encourage an often discouraged author. I owe an extra debt of gratitude to Jeff Stout, who brought this project to the attention of The Pennsylvania State University Press. During that same year, I received generous and thoughtful advice from Henry Levinson and Douglas Langston, two astute critics of my work and work habits.

At a very crucial stage in the evolution of this work, the original manuscript came to the attention of Stephen Crites and Hans Frei. The painstaking and voluminous written comments offered me by each of these uncommon scholars constituted a major turning point for me. My gratitude to them both is as profound as it is humbling.

Finally, others who have read and commented on my work—or otherwise helped to keep me thinking clearly about faith and history—include my father, Gordon Michalson, and Heiko Oberman, John Macquarrie, Richard Young, George Hall, and Robert Morgan. My students at Oberlin, besides exhibiting great patience in listening to me talk endlessly about problems of faith and history, have, through their comments and questions, given me deeper insight into my topic. And Philip Winsor and Patricia A. Coryell of The Pennsylvania State University Press have helped to bring this project to its final stages with the utmost efficiency and good judgment.

I hope that all of these friends and colleagues find the finished product interesting and useful, even where they may disagree with its contents or point of view.

1
Introduction

It sometimes happens, in philosophy, that a whole set of distinct problems so resemble one another that a greater care than philosophers are willing to exercise is required to keep them apart. But because all these problems are treated as one, and because considerations which might properly bear upon one of them, are mingled together with considerations which might properly bear upon another, a satisfactory solution to either of them becomes increasingly difficult, and a vast and tangled and singularly frustrating philosophical literature grows up.

—Arthur Danto, "The Historical Individual"

LESSING'S "UGLY DITCH"

An image or a metaphor, although introduced almost casually, sometimes takes on a life of its own, insuring a measure of immortality for its inventor. This appears to be the case with an image proposed over 200 years ago by Gotthold Ephraim Lessing:

> If no historical truth can be demonstrated, then nothing can be demonstrated by means of historical truths. That is: Accidental truths of history can never become the proof of necessary truths of reason. . . . That, then, is the ugly, broad ditch which I cannot get across, however often and however earnestly I have tried to make the leap.[1]

Lessing's "ugly ditch," if not the most frequently cited nonbiblical image within Protestant theology during the past two centuries, is certainly in the running for that dubious title. Part of the reason, no doubt, is that Lessing offers us, not a dry abstraction, difficult to decipher, but a genuine and straightforward picture: we see two reaches of earth, separated by a divide of open space.

But further details of this picture will vary from imagination to imagination. The ditch may be wide or narrow, shallow or deep. It may be a minor disruption in an otherwise smooth and continuous plain, or it may wind and stretch for many miles, like the trenches of a World War I battlefield. The opposing sides of the ditch might differ widely in their steepness, symmetry, and general conformation. It may be a ditch that we can straddle, or one—like Lessing's—that we must try to leap. Perhaps, on the other hand, it will be a ditch too wide and too dangerously deep for either.

References to the ugly ditch typically crop up as a kind of code or shorthand signaling "the problem" of faith and history. Yet these references often fail to do justice to the potential differences in detail that different thinkers, with very different theological imaginations, might bring with them to the elementary picture. Often, the standard assumption prevailing in discussions of these matters is that there is one problem coming to expression through Lessing's idiom, one that requires some kind of leap for its successful resolution, due to a nagging dualism or hiatus. Lessing himself, of course, due in part (he tells us) to his "old legs" and his "heavy head,"[2] could not make it across. Kierkegaard, who would make the ditch famous, comes along and leaps. In both cases, the difficulty concerns the transition from the mere accidents or contingencies of history, associated especially with the life and career of Jesus, to the assurances of religious faith. Because historical truths are always only accidental, this problem has chiefly to do with successfully coping with the lingering element of uncertainty present in even the most secure historical knowledge; thereupon, faith might feel free of the troublesome possibility that it must "change with every new consensus of New Testament criticism or hold its breath lest some discovery in the Dead Sea area casts a shadow of doubt over this or that particular belief."[3] Kierkegaard, in a variation on a fundamentally Kantian theme, saves modern Protestantism by showing that authentic faith has nothing to do with the acceptance of historical facts anyway. And, although it is Lessing who poses the problem in such memorable fashion, it is Kierkegaard whose solution would be most influential.

Same ditch, two different responses—or so it seems.

Unfortunately, the position occupied by Lessing's image within modern theology is far more complicated than this standard overview would suggest. The real situation is more like the mixed results we would get upon asking everyone in a roomful of people to fill in the specific details of our basic, collective picture of a ditch. Not even Lessing and Kierkegaard themselves agree on what the image should finally look like. The real situation, in other words, is: different responses to different ditches.

What follows is a philosophical exploration aimed at untangling the several different issues conveyed by the deceptively straightforward dualism of Lessing's image. As we shall quickly learn, the problem is not simply that the ditch can be conveniently appropriated to mean any number of things, depending upon the theological needs of the moment. Instead, the problem begins with Lessing himself who, it turns out, is not talking about one ditch at all, but three, all three of which continue to haunt Protestant theology. And, as though to guarantee confusion in subsequent discussions of theology and history, Lessing manages within the space of his brief essay to alternate his allusions to the several different problems with the most unpredictable arbitrariness, prompting Samuel Taylor Coleridge, an astute reader of Lessing's essay, to observe: "I feel at each reperusal more and more puzzled how so palpable a *miss* could have been made by so acute a mind."[4]

Coleridge may or may not have been taking into account the notorious slipperiness of Lessing in religious matters. As Hans Frei has recently put it, Lessing was "remarkably ironic in his treatment of religious themes as soon as controversy moved close to an inquiry into his own views of Christianity. He carefully covered his tracks and was much clearer about what he was against than what he was for."[5] No small part of what follows will be devoted to sorting out the ambiguities in Lessing's own discussion. But whatever we, along with Coleridge, might conclude about Lessing's consistency, there can be no question that his timing was excellent. In the most economical fashion, he conveys in a single image the difficulties that an emerging historical consciousness would increasingly pose to Christian theology during the following two centuries. Indeed, problems connected with history perhaps constitute the very center of Protestant theological reflection and debate since Lessing's time. Certainly this is suggested both by a roster of names that includes Hegel and Baur, Strauss and Bultmann, Schweitzer and Troeltsch, and by such specific developments as two separate quests of the historical Jesus, the emergence of a history-of-religions approach to Christian origins, and fresh views of scripture produced by form and redaction criticism. If Lessing leaves behind him a confusing and ambiguous legacy, theological developments since his time suggest that this is probably to his credit.

LESSING'S DITCH AND
MODERN PROTESTANT THOUGHT

Because it involves several problems and not one, the image of the ugly ditch occupies a number of different locations within modern

Protestant theology. As the influence of both Lessing and Kierkegaard on this point would suggest, its most prominent location is
within theological discussions of historical knowledge. Given the
apparent reliance of Christian faith upon reference to historical
events, Lessing struck a raw nerve when he underscored the now
familiar claim that the truths of history are merely "accidental." In
his own elaboration of Lessing's problem, Kierkegaard would accentuate just this point by maintaining that, even at best, historical
knowledge is always "mere approximation knowledge." Even "the
most masterly historical elucidation is only the most masterly 'as
good as,' an almost," Kierkegaard tells us.[6]

For good reason, we have gradually become more Kierkegaardian
than even Kierkegaard on this point. Wilhelm Herrmann (whose
influence as teacher of both Barth and Bultmann would have a
significant impact on twentieth-century theology) suggests that "no
historical judgment, however certain it may appear, ever attains
anything more than probability."

> But what sort of a religion would that be which accepted a basis for its
> convictions with the consciousness that it was only probably safe? For
> this reason, it is impossible to attach religious conviction to a mere
> historical decision. Here Lessing is right.[7]

Herrmann's solution to the difficulty raised by Lessing—a solution
based on a dubious appeal to the "inner life" of Jesus as the true
ground of faith[8]—set the pattern for more recent strategies for dealing with the mere probabilities of historical research. Like Martin
Kähler's invocation of the distinction between the *historisch* and the
geschichtlich in his polemical response to the life-of-Jesus movement,[9] Herrmann's appeal to the inner life of Jesus exploited a
fundamentally Kantian dualism that allowed Christian faith to hide
behind a noumenal wall, safe from the ravages of historical inquiry.
Whatever the flaws intrinsic to these sorts of efforts to salvage both
faith and christology in the face of historical criticism, it is noteworthy that claims about the corrigible and shifting character of historical knowledge set both the tone and the context of these theological maneuvers. The search for that notorious *sturmfreies Gebiet*—
a region where faith is entirely insulated from the results of ongoing
historical research—makes sense only when historical knowledge is
thought to be an unworthy partner for faith.[10]

The long career of Bultmann constitutes the full and final deployment of this dualistic strategy for neutralizing the effects of historical

criticism. Bultmann's early training in the atmosphere of theological liberalism, as well as his own adoption of a history-of-religions approach to Christian origins, produced in him a keen awareness of the epistemological issues attending modern historiography. His existentialist variation on Kähler's distinction between the "Jesus of history" and the "Christ of faith" would be Bultmann's way of indulging his profound admiration for the critical element in liberal Protestantism,[11] while simultaneously enjoying the advantages of a *sturmfreies Gebiet* for faith and christology. As in the cases of both Herrmann and Kähler, Bultmann's entire program would thus be undertaken in the full conviction that Lessing was correct about the character of historical knowledge and about the relation between faith and historical results. Historical research, Bultmann tells us in a characteristic comment, "can never lead to any result which could serve as a basis for faith, for *all its results have only relative validity.*"[12] History, so it seems, can only offer us knowledge that is more or less probable, often fragmentary, and always subject to future change and correction. Consequently, Bultmann concludes in a clear echo of Kierkegaard, Christian faith "does not at all arise from the acceptance of historical facts."[13]

Such a result, of course, has been extremely convenient for modern theology, not simply because of the troublesome epistemology of history underscored by Lessing, Kierkegaard, Herrmann, and Bultmann, but also because of the largely negative results of much historical-critical work into biblical materials conducted during the modern era. Yet, however convenient it may be, the broadly Bultmannian and radically dualistic solution to Lessing's ditch has never represented a full consensus and continues to have its detractors. For some, such as Wolfhart Pannenberg, the Bultmannian positon eliminates the genuinely cognitive and objective element that rightfully belongs to the confession of faith, and thereby produces an illicit subjectivizing of faith for which Kierkegaard and ultimately even Kant are to blame.[14] The effect is to misunderstand completely the role that historical judgments do and must play in support of faith. For others, on the other hand, the familiar assertion that faith is independent of historical research is all-too-often accompanied by faith claims that covertly introduce historical judgments unaccounted for by modern critical procedures. Such an illicit move, according to this line of criticism, was already present in Herrmann's appeal to the inner life of Jesus, and remains, in one form or another, in the several variations of dialectical or neo-orthodox theology dominating reflection on faith and history during the first half of our own century. The Bultmannian presumption that theology is free from the results of historical research often goes hand-in-hand with a covert reliance on claims that are rightfully open to historiographical adjudication. The result, in Van Harvey's characterization, is an unacceptable clash between two different "moralities of knowledge," the classic impasse between the secular historian and the traditional believer.[15]

Even some who are in profound sympathy with the Bultmannian position, such as James Robinson, suggest that Bultmann violates the possibilities inherent in his own position by introducing an unacceptable hiatus between the Jesus of history and the Christ of the kerygma.[16] Drawing explicitly on the same existentialist historiography presumably employed by Bultmann himself, Robinson argues that "in encountering Jesus one is confronted with the same existential decision as that posed by the kerygma" about the risen Christ.[17] According to this view, Bultmann's insistence upon a break between the Jesus of history and the Christ of faith insinuates that the kerygma's reference to Jesus of Nazareth is not a fitting one.[18] If it *is* a fitting reference, however, then the same understanding of existence must be present in the historical Jesus as in the early Christian kerygma. This claim is supposedly made more plausible by Robinson's reminder that an existential self-understanding is not equivalent to self-consciousness, a fine distinction that presumably helps Robinson's "new quest" of the historical Jesus to avoid certain problems associated with the old quest: existentialist historiography does not require that the theologian discover what the historical Jesus consciously thought about himself.[19] To argue in reply, as does Bultmann, that the historical Jesus was a Jew, who cannot be viewed in material continuity with the kerygmatic witness, is, claims Robinson, unaccountably to fall back into the categories of the history-of-religions school and to abandon the existentialist categories that Bultmann himself had put on the theological map. A refined Bultmannian historiography, rid of this troubling equivocation, will necessarily take a genuinely theological interest in the historical Jesus himself.[20]

In one form or another, these responses to Bultmannian fashions find their point of departure in commentary about historical method. Such cases, and many others like them, suggest that the problem of historical knowledge and its relation to theology remains an unsettled and highly problematic issue. In this form, certainly, Lessing's ugly ditch is still very much with us.

But the problem of historical knowledge and its relation to faith and theology is not the issue that is most pressing for Lessing himself or for his most influential successor and commentator, Kierkegaard. However prominent their famous references to the "accidental" and "approximate" character of historical knowledge may be, we are misled in thinking that Lessing and Kierkegaard are primarily worried about the corrigibility of historical results. This concern is in fact secondary for them both; historiographical and epistemological issues occasionally veil the more profound difficulties at stake in their consideration of the ugly ditch. The possibility arises that, not only do we invoke the image of Lessing's ditch in careless and confusing ways, but we give historiographical and epistemological issues an unwarranted degree of importance in discussions of theology and history.

It is against the background of such problems as these that I undertake this untangling of the overlapping issues conveyed by Lessing's image. The inquiry itself might best be thought of as a kind of anatomy, if—with *Webster's*—we understand that term to mean "a separating or dividing into parts for detailed examination."[21] The sheer process of sorting will, I believe, justify itself in its very execution. Yet if there is one point which deserves emphasis from the very outset, it is that, beginning with Lessing himself, discussions of the nature of the ditch and of theological strategies for dealing with it have been haunted by a simple equivocation concerning the word *history:* sometimes the aim is to refer to a type of *event;* while at other times the aim is to consider a type of *knowledge.* As my preceding account has already suggested, our own view of both Lessing and Kierkegaard on this matter highlights the knowledge, or epistemological, aspect—historical *knowledge* is somehow untrustworthy or suspect, producing the often-cited incommensurability between Christian faith and historical research. Furthermore, the character of historical-critical developments since Kierkegaard's time has given us good reason to keep our attention focused on this epistemological aspect, as exemplified by the work and influence of Bultmann.

However, the careful reading of Lessing and Kierkegaard prompted by a reexamination of the ugly ditch reveals that the very real impasse for them between faith and history has nothing to do with the character of historical knowledge. Comments about historical knowledge may help to structure their discussions of the problem, but their characterizations of historical knowledge are derivative from, and not constitutive of, their true reasons for identifying a problem in the first place. As we shall see, the deeper problem for them both is more closely associated with the category of historical revelation than with the epistemology of history. Here, then, is the chief moral of the inquiry: by the time Lessing and Kierkegaard get around to characterizing historical knowledge, all the important things have already been decided. Such lessons as this moral offers to contemporary discussions of theology and history will, I trust, become clear in the course of the total inquiry.

THE TEMPORAL PROBLEM

I have indicated that Lessing actually exposes three different ditches, and not merely one. By this I mean that his discussion in "On the Proof of the Spirit and of Power" touches on three separate problem areas, each of which involves a "gap" or a divide that finds appropriate expression in the image of the ditch. These three problems are: (1) the "temporal gap" separating the present from religiously momentous or revelatory events of the distant past, which is where the specific issue of historical reconstruction resides, together with related problems of evidence, testimony, probability, and proof; (2) the "metaphysical gap" between historical truths and religious truths, a gap that can assume several different forms depending upon the sense in which we take the word *history* here, as well as upon our initial theological commitments; and (3) the "existential gap" that potentially separates a modern-day, autonomous, and secular believer from a religious message that is not only historically dubious, but probably odd and incredible as well. Each of these problems is intimately related to the other two. At the same time, however, each is distinctive in important respects and deserves separate treatment.

Lessing himself introduces the first problem, that of temporal distance from revelatory historical events, by his distinction between miracles and fulfilled prophecies "which I myself experience," and those "of which I know only from history that others say they have experienced them."[22] The issue here concerns the problem of sufficient historical evidence for the truth of religious beliefs, a topic which generated lively debate during the eighteenth century. In a manner typical of such debates, Lessing frames the issue in a way that makes religious truths appear to be potentially capable of "proof"—this, after all, is the point of the cumbersome title of his essay.[23] Consequently, the issue at stake in connection with the temporal gap is the question of whether or not certain historical events actually occurred, the religious meaning of which is presumably obvious and straightforward.

Lessing appears to be making two important assumptions. First, he assumes that firsthand experience is qualitatively superior to reliance on someone else's testimony and can serve as the firm basis of religious conviction. Second, he assumes that events of a certain sort convey their religious meaning clearly and unambiguously. Lessing's discussion of the problem of temporal distance thereby creates the initial impression that the chief difficulty to be explored in his essay is the dependence of the modern-day believer upon accurate historical reconstruction of the events in question. If Lessing's main concern is both the advantage enjoyed by the original eyewitness and the disadvantage suffered by a later generation of potential believers, then the goal of the later generation becomes historical reconstruction that most closely approximates the ideal of firsthand experience. Underlying this is the implication that historical "proofs" are religiously germane. Yet if the necessary historical reconstruction is missing or, for some reason, impossible, then the present-day believer has a real problem.

There is a basically empiricist cast to the issue of temporal distance, since the ideal of firsthand experience is presumed to be without serious epistemic difficulties that would bear on religious matters. And the several philosophical issues attending this aspect of Lessing's ditch constitute a familiar empiricist cluster: the question of sufficient evidence; the role of testimony in the fashioning of beliefs; and the role played by probability in the construction of the historical record. How sure can I be that the testimony I have received from others is accurate? What if earlier witnesses testify to an event—such as a miracle or a fulfilled prophecy—for which I enjoy no analogue in my own experience? Does not historical inquiry always produce, even at best, a record of the past that is only "more or less" accurate and is forever open to change and correction? Can historical research ever yield a result that is the epistemological equivalent of firsthand experience? If not, am I not condemned to a religious faith that is always tentative and provisional?

The issue of temporal distance, then, is fundamentally a problem concerning the difference between a contemporary and a noncontemporary of historical revelation. It is in terms of the idiom of contemporaneity that Kierkegaard will also pursue this issue. Moreover, the problem of temporal distance is implicit in more recent theological anxieties about the relative, fragmentary, or otherwise mixed results of historical inquiry into matters of religious relevance, anxieties that are often framed in terms of Kierkegaard's own notion of historical knowledge as "mere approximation knowledge."

However, as we shall see, the temporal issue is basically a red herring in Lessing's discussion: as it turns out, nothing of religious significance is produced whether or not accurate historical reconstruction actually occurs. Likewise, Kierkegaard introduces the contemporaneity theme mainly to demonstrate the religious *insignificance* of firsthand experience. But if firsthand experience offers no religious advantage, then difficulties of historical reconstruction must not be the chief problem posed by the ditch for Kierkegaard any more than for Lessing. Kierkegaard's comments about historical research always yielding mere approximation knowledge are misunderstood if they are taken to mean that the assurances of firsthand experience are religiously efficacious, or even if they are taken to be the basis of the Kierkegaardian incommensurability between Christian faith and historical knowledge. For Kierkegaard, true discipleship turns out to have nothing to do with being an eyewitness. And if Lessing and Kierkegaard are accurate guides in these matters, all of this suggests that more recent theological discussions of historical method and of the presuppositions of historical inquiry are potentially misleading. Modern nervousness about historical reconstruction would be roughly equivalent to Lessing's complaint about the hazards of relying on the testimony of others. But this is to make the problem of the ditch a basically factual problem, turning on the nature and results of empirical inquiry. And, as Lessing and Kierkegaard go on to show us, the chief difficulty for them is not a factual one at all.

THE METAPHYSICAL PROBLEM

As we shall see, Lessing abruptly shifts from a focus on temporal distance to a concern about two different classes of truths. Here we confront our second major problem area, which involves the incommensurability between particular historical truths on the one hand, and dogmatic religious truths of a presumably universal significance on the other. This is not a temporal problem at all, but a metaphysical one that is time invariant.

In his own essay, Lessing broaches the metaphysical topic at three different levels, but without ever sorting them out. There is, first, the question that is latent in and continuous throughout his essay, concerning whether a contingent and unique historical revelation, upon which all religious truth and human salvation rely, is an inherently rational or a religiously necessary idea. Part of the Lessing we meet in "On the Proof of the Spirit and of Power" is thereby wrestling with the "scandal of particularity" that rests at the center of Enlightenment debates over revealed and natural religion. Like other important religious thinkers of the eighteenth and early nineteenth centuries, Lessing is here attempting to come to terms with the so-called problem of positivity, which typically involves reliance on a definite historical revelation or a divine intrusion as the source of theological authority. The positivity issue is closely related, but not identical to, the problem of miracle and the category of the supernatural.[24] It is more fundamentally related to the general problem of reason and revelation and to associated difficulties, still very much with us, concerning the competing demands of divine authority and human autonomy.

The sheer intelligibility of a historical revelation is not the only form in which Lessing injects a metaphysical gap into his discussion. For, second, he advances the metaphysical issue with a logical twist, reflected in his often-quoted comment about using "accidental truths of history" as the "proof of necessary truths of reason." Here we confront the important role played in this essay by the Leibnizian distinction between contingent and necessary truths. As employed by Lessing, this distinction categorizes historical claims according to their logical status, while simultaneously exposing Lessing's own rationalist predilections in religious affairs. Insofar as it does the latter, it reveals both the artificiality and the dispensability of Lessing's concerns about the temporal ditch. If, ultimately, a rational principle is in religious control, then nothing important really depends upon any form of factual inquiry, historical or otherwise. In other words, Lessing's eventual subordination of contingency to necessity in religious matters makes dispensable his initial concern about temporal distance. Truths of reason are not affected by matters of fact.

Third, Lessing complains about moving from even the most assured historical results—to which he would, for purposes of argument, submit—to orthodox christological claims. This incommensurability *seems* to be the same issue as the one involved in the distinction between contingent and necessary truths, except for the fact that christological claims are not necessary truths. They are, to be sure, radically different from normal historical assertions; but they are also distinct from the concept of necessity conveyed by Lessing's Leibnizian formula. The contingency-necessity distinction does not exhaust the class of theologically significant utterances, even within Lessing's own essay.

Thus, the metaphysical problem introduced by Lessing's ditch concerns (1) the very rationality of the idea of a particular historical moment serving as the basis of human salvation; (2) the distance between contingent and necessary truths, which will be most pressing for those with a stake in philosophical necessity; and (3) the distance between historical claims and dogmatic propositions of a non-necessary sort. Again, Kierkegaard will address all of these themes, and it is just here that he drastically transforms Lessing's problem into an entirely fresh set of issues. As we shall see, this is primarily because his views on the positivity issue are the exact opposite of Lessing's: the "project of thought" constituting Kierkegaard's *Philosophical Fragments* is, in effect, an intentionally abstract device for reversing the general position on reason and revelation evident in Lessing and his idealist successors.

Furthermore, Kierkegaard will give careful attention to the relationship between contingent and necessary truths. But unlike Lessing, who attends to this issue because of his religious stake in necessity, Kierkegaard turns to it because of his religious stake in the contingencies of history: his position on the positivity issue dovetails with his need to elicit from history the free and unnecessitated act of God in the incarnation. At the same time, Kierkegaard offers us a far more detailed and nuanced account than does Lessing of the crucial difference between history as a type of event, and history as a type of knowledge, even though he is, at times, as capable as Lessing of trading on the ambiguity of the term.

Finally, Kierkegaard rejects the concept of necessity as the appropriate category for thinking through the christological issue. For Lessing, Jesus is religiously important only to the extent that he embodies or somehow brings to expression truths that are not contingent upon his historical appearance. Thus, the contingency-necessity distinction not only informs Lessing's view of historical truth, but it underwrites any truly religious interest he might have in Jesus: with respect to history, the contingency side of the distinction plays the determining role; with respect to christology, the notion of necessary truth is decisive. This of course means, however, that the religious significance of Jesus does not reside in the sheer contingent or accidental "eventful-ness" of his historical appearance. Lessing will not base his religious interest in Jesus on the contingent fact *that* he lived, but on the connection between Jesus and religious truths that are necessarily binding whether or not Jesus ever lived.

Kierkegaard refuses to locate the point of christology in philo-sophical necessity. The contingency-necessity distinction is useful to him primarily as a basis for eliminating necessity from the histori-cal realm; achieving this is a chief goal of the anti-Hegelianism that influences Kierkegaard's authorship in powerful ways. He will thus argue that, if we are to speak accurately of the dilemma facing the believer whose faith is connected to a past event, we find ourselves confronting a distinction different from that between contingency and necessity—which is to say, we find ourselves confronting a ditch that is different from Lessing's. Kierkegaard's version of Lessing's ditch is ultimately rendered, not in terms of the contrast between contingent, historical truth and *necessity*, but in terms of the very different contrast between contingent, historical truth and *eternity*.[25] And in this formula—which commentators seem inexplicably eager simply to equate with Lessing's[26]—Kierkegaard poses the dilemma of successfully relating history to christology in a deeper way. For in the Kierkegaardian version, the contingent historical appearance of Jesus becomes decisive precisely in its "eventful" character, and not as the illustration of something else. Successfully relating contin-gency to eternity, rather than to necessity, thereby requires peculiar new categories (such as "paradox") that account for the relationship between Jesus and history. The convenient solution of rendering this relationship in the rational terms provided by a mediating theory of philosophical necessity is simply not available. The "eventful" char-acter of Jesus' appearance remains a stumbling block to reasoning of that sort.

Between them, Lessing and Kierkegaard thus touch on all three elements of the metaphysical aspect of the ditch. The roles played by these three elements in subsequent Protestant theology have varied widely, and it is precisely here that certain problems in dis-cussions of faith, history, and revelation have developed during the past century. Especially within debates connected with the work of Bultmann, the issue of history and its relation to christology is often combined in confusing and unacknowledged ways with the issue of positivity. More confusing still, discussions of historical knowledge and the problem of historical skepticism are sometimes injected into these matters as though the temporal ditch is the main diffi-culty—as though, in other words, firsthand experience is the ideal of faith, however unattainable it may be. But in a setting where even the iron-clad assurances of firsthand experience would yield no theological dividend, introducing the temporal difficulty can only confuse, not clarify. As we shall see by the end of this study, to locate a confusion of this sort is probably to locate an excessive and misleading preoccupation with historiographical difficulties, one that inflates the importance of such difficulties for theology.

THE PROBLEM OF RELIGIOUS APPROPRIATION

Finally, Lessing presents us with a gap separating the modern-day believer from a potentially peculiar or even incredible religious message. This gap suggests the difficult problem of religious "appropriation," particularly as this problem involves the conditions necessary for an individual's successfully apprehending, accepting, and perhaps even understanding the religious message. In our own time, this difficulty can be accurately rendered as the "existential ditch," due to the sheer hiatus between myself and my natural store of self-knowledge, and the alien religious message that may be a scandal or an affront to my normal sensibilities. Such a hiatus, apparently unamenable at the rational level of conceptual mediation, calls instead for a "leap."

Obviously, the appropriation issue is an expression of the general problem of "plausibility" within modern theology. During the last 100 years or so, this difficulty has not been made any simpler by the discovery that, to use Schweitzer's expression, Jesus himself comes as a "stranger" to us.[27] Thus, the appropriation issue can be focused more specifically in terms of the deceptively straightforward question: "Does Jesus have any genuine relevance for the modern man or woman?"—a question fundamentally transformed by the discovery of the eschatological character of Jesus and his message. From this standpoint, modern efforts to "existentialize" or otherwise domesticate even eschatology itself reflect on the needs and intentions of recent theology in telling ways. Moreover, given the general assortment of peculiar difficulties connected with the appropriation issue, it is no wonder that the category of "paradox," together with fresh conceptions of what constitutes true "contemporaneity," have been at the very center of modern Protestant reflection on the nature of faith. Nor, from a somewhat broader perspective, is it surprising to witness the transformation of the formal mode of modern Protestant theology from *Dogmatik* to *Glaubenslehre*.

In certain respects, the gap setting up the appropriation problem is the dominating theme in Lessing's "On the Proof of the Spirit and of Power," since the one general issue connecting the various parts of this confusing essay may well be the problem of personally appropriating a religious message that is somehow dubious, strange, or fantastic. But this theme dominates only "in certain respects," for it is not altogether clear that Lessing recognizes the appropriation issue for what it is. Lessing is shrewd enough to sense that there is indeed a problem here, but he does not quite have the conceptual tools for spelling out the problem in its truly modern form or for dealing with it in a straightforward manner. Again, at issue here is the idea that a message recalling remote events occurring in the backwaters of the Mediterranean world could possibly have a bearing on a genuinely autonomous man or woman. For the most part, Lessing is dealing with this issue in terms of the sheer credibility of the events under consideration; he is, in other words, dealing with the appropriation problem largely in the terms provided by the deist controversies and by eighteenth-century debates over the various "evidences" for the truth of Christianity.[28]

But if this were all that Lessing was doing here, then what I am calling the appropriation issue would simply be a variation on the temporal ditch. This is because the accent would fall exclusively on the question of the reliability of reports about religiously momentous historical events. However, something else is indeed going on, which is signaled in particular by Lessing's use of the metaphor of truths that are "binding," and by his fairly explicit limitation of authentic religious truths to those that can be described in terms of this metaphor.

> But since the truth of these miracles has completely ceased to be demonstrable by miracles happening now, since they are no more than reports of miracles . . . , I deny that they can and should bind me to the very least faith in the other teachings of Christ.

> What then does bind me? Nothing but these teachings themselves.[29]

Lurking in the metaphor of binding is the theme of human autonomy. Lessing intimates the appropriation problem in its modern form by demanding that the religious message, coming out of the past, strike at least a chord of recognition in the believer, if not automatic assent. The religious message cannot be binding on the believer simply because of the authority of scripture or church, for then I should be victimized by heteronomy, a sure mark, for Lessing, of false religion. As in the case of his polemical interchange with Johann Goeze, subsequent to Lessing's publication of the "Fragments" of Reimarus, repudiating the appeal to unquestioned authority in the settlement of a religious question is the chief issue in

Lessing's mind. The implicit alternative—never fully worked out by Lessing—is to locate a mediating point of contact between the believer and the religious message, a point where there is an immediate, intuitive "fit" between the two. The authentic religious message is binding, and religious appropriation thus occurs, because of a latent connection between what the message contains and what I as potential believer bring with me in the form of some inherent feature or dimension of my religious self. The message finally "makes sense" because of this implicit harmony between myself and the wider moral-religious universe of which I am a part, and which is reflected in the authentic religious message. This theme, worked out more fully by Lessing in his play, *Nathan the Wise*, reflects his ultimate appeal to the "inner truth"[30] of religion, which he, like other Enlightenment thinkers, construes in basically moral terms. As the theme of religious tolerance in that play clearly shows, the notion of inner truth is intimately connected to the idea of the universality of authentic religion, a criterion that pervades Enlightenment rationalism in profound ways.

Like countless successors in this task of evidencing the truth of Christianity by first showing its personal meaning, Lessing seeks out a means of accounting for our appropriation of religious claims that does for an enlightened era what the unproblematic reference to the work of the Holy Spirit achieved for an earlier one. He is probably trying to capture, in a more sophisticated form, the simple, heartfelt religiosity of the Moravian pietism that always impressed him more than either Lutheran orthodoxy or the halfway house in which the neologians of his day had landed.[31] But in his efforts to articulate and respond to the appropriation problem, Lessing is also pointing the way toward later developments of great importance, characteristic of the German idealists and Schleiermacher. The key issue is the so-called point of contact between believer and religious message. Prior to the appearance of Kant and, especially, Hegel, it was no doubt impossible to articulate the issue of religious appropriation in its truly modern form. Too much depends upon the profoundly new theory of the self, and particularly the relationship between selfhood and temporality, that emerge at the very end of the eighteenth century.

Lessing represents a stage in this development of a new view of the religious self—if he is not an actual precursor of the idealists—because of his appeal to the inner truth of authentic religion. The metaphor itself signals the modern turn "inward," into the recesses of the self, in search of the true basis of religious appropriation.

Again, the governing principle here—as in the case of the metaphor of "binding"—is human autonomy and the requirement that authentic religion do justice to the autonomous self. The chief consequence of this principle for the issue of historical revelation constitutes a clear paradigm shift in religious matters: the religious message scores its point because of something that was "in me" all along and not because of something in an "outer" message, associated with historical events, that is binding on me in heteronomous ways. The autonomous self gradually becomes the criterion for what can be considered truly revelatory.

This shift of emphasis away from the outer message and toward the inner self does not occur without significant alterations in the message itself. For even Lessing's theory of religious appropriation, based upon an initial accounting of an aspect of personal existence or consciousness, succeeds only at the cost of rendering the distinctively *historical* feature of the religious message potentially dispensable and even irrelevant. History simply becomes the vehicle for disclosing truths of a fundamentally nonhistorical character. In this respect, the line from Lessing runs illuminatingly through Kant, Strauss, and the demythologizing movement of our own era.

The puzzling way in which Kierkegaard figures into these matters accounts for much of the complexity of more recent Protestant thought, which has been so heavily influenced by him. Kierkegaard reverses Lessing's stand on the positivity issue and stresses a particular historical moment as the decisive source of truth and salvation. Without just *that* historical moment, Kierkegaard is saying, Christian faith has no point; the scandal of particularity will not be mitigated by the pretensions of natural theology. At the same time, however, Kierkegaard joins Lessing in inflating the role played by the subject of faith in his account of religious appropriation. Even though his position appears to require the endorsement of a certain historical event as the very center of faith, Kierkegaard has no more desire than does Lessing to make assent to matters of historical detail a prerequisite for discipleship. As a result, subjective appropriation takes the place of considerations of historical detail in Kierkegaard's own anatomy of the ditch and its problems. Indeed, far more than even Lessing, Kierkegaard forces the appropriation issue to center stage, leaving behind any serious concern for matters of historical fact.

This is partly because Kierkegaard, in sharp contrast to Lessing, offers no skeptical qualms about the historical content of faith— about the "what" of Christianity. But because of his unparalleled preoccupation with the "how" of Christianity—with, that is, the problem of how the individual actually becomes a Christian—Kierkegaard leaves behind a legacy that bears in peculiar ways on a generation no longer complacent about the historical "what." Thus, particularly in existentialist theological circles, the presumably negative effects of historical criticism have been rendered tolerable by engineering a displacement of the traditional, historical content of faith by the increasingly sophisticated mechanics of religious appropriation: theology gradually becomes hermeneutical, virtually without remainder. Retreat from reliance on a historical referent of faith that was an unproblematic object of belief for an earlier orthodoxy is made theologically respectable by rendering apparently historical claims into propositions of a self-referential sort. History is replaced by historicity. Even in Kierkegaard himself, the genuinely historical content of faith, seemingly required by his position on the positivity issue, begins to fade from view and to reside in a mere vanishing point. Serious questions arise concerning the articulation of the *content* of faith in other than purely self-referential terms. For certainly one key feature of twentieth-century existentialist theology, represented most of all by Bultmann and his followers, has been an increasing amorphousness concerning "that which is believed by faith" (the *fides quae creditur*), in contrast to increasingly refined accounts of the existential act or resolve of the subject of faith (the *fides qua creditur*). The irony, to employ terms suggested by the present inquiry, is crystallized in Bultmann himself, in whom we have Kierkegaardian reliance on reference to a past event (the "act of God" in the cross-resurrection sequence[32]), joined together with a reductionistic approach to history worthy of Lessing himself (that is, demythologization). The resulting loss of interest in a public historical content as a part of faith's confession is not simply characteristic of Bultmann, but is a key motif in the story of Protestant theology from Schleiermacher to such "left-wing" Bultmannians as Fritz Buri and Wilhelm Kamlah—a story that not only has several possible interpretations, but one that has still to be played out.

In this connection, it is of more than passing interest that, toward the end of his own career, Bultmann had to defend his position against those—such as Kamlah[33]—who would eliminate even the one remaining reference to history decisive for him in the rendering of faith. Significantly, a willingness to demythologize even Bultmann's "act of God" potentially makes "faith" possible apart from reference to Jesus.[34] In Bultmann's left-wing critics, in other words, we come full circle back to the position of Lessing. For any attempt to subordinate what comes to expression in Jesus to what can be known, apprehended, or existentially actualized apart from reference to him is a tacit admission that Lessing and his idealist tradition are right, and that the "eventful" character of historical revelation is dispensable and is the appropriate target of reductionism. Certainly the several contemporary efforts to expose areas of overlap between Christian faith and modern secularity's "basic faith" or confidence in the meaning and value of human existence are worth considering in light of this wider problem of reason and revelation.[35] The dilemma is much the same today as in Lessing's time: it concerns weighing the distinctiveness of Christian faith over against its intelligibility.[36] To tilt too far toward the former is to risk remaining in an intellectual ghetto, with no lines of communication between faith and the surrounding culture. But to tilt too far toward the latter is to risk robbing the adjective *Christian* of any real point or meaning—it might almost be to turn Christian apologetics into something like a revisionary Marxism that holds that capitalism is the true "inner meaning" of Marxism.[37] After all, it seems true that if we stress long and loud enough the changes in the *meaning* of a language we once took literally, we are at some point signaling fundamental changes in our *beliefs* as well.[38]

In their own efforts to deal with the problem of religious appropriation, Lessing and Kierkegaard thus leave us with an important theological moral. This concerns the apparent triumph of the so-called subject of faith within much modern Protestant reflection on faith, history, and revelation. This retreat from theological reliance on statements of historical fact is naturally accompanied by a severe constriction of the assertorial element in the Christian confession, leading some critics to wonder aloud if Christian faith might be compatible with any state of affairs whatever. In scholastic terminology, the point is that the element of *notitia* in religious knowing is swallowed up by an increasingly magnified element of *fiducia*. Theological interest in the outer world of public history is displaced by a preoccupation with the inner world of personal selfhood or consciousness; developments in theology oddly recapitulate the new orientation toward the private self occurring in the culture generally.

Potentially, the only true "knowing" that occurs in faith then is a form of *self*-knowledge or apprehension. For some, of course, this self-referential feature represents precisely the point of a conception of faith come of age, suggesting our final emancipation from an outmoded world view and the litmus test of a theology worthy of serious consideration. For others, however, led by Barth, the triumph of the subject is a case of Cartesian chickens coming home to roost: the consequence is the forfeiture of an authentic dogmatics through a trivializing preoccupation with the "appropriate conceptuality" for doing proper theology.

From such a standpoint as this, the current malaise within Protestant theology—characterized especially by a preoccupation with "methodology" and "foundations," as well as by the motif of the "alienated theologian"[39]—is the inevitable result of a series of wrong turns. The cumulative effect of these wrong turns is to make it difficult, if not impossible, to frame questions regarding history and revelation in the right way. And if this is the situation we face, then the proper task of theology is not to generate one more highly technical solution to the problem of Lessing's ditch. Instead, the proper task is to eliminate the conceptual framework serving as the context for the wrong questions about history and revelation. The possibility arises that ditch imagery itself may be *part* of the problem, and not a *description* of some other problem.

OVERVIEW OF THE INQUIRY

It should go without saying that I can hardly hope to offer an exhaustive and fully documented account of all of these issues in a study of relatively modest length. Nor will I be attempting to say very much about Lessing that goes beyond his notorious essay, or about Kierkegaard that goes beyond his Johannes Climacus writings. The chief aim of this study, as I indicated at the outset, is to untangle and demarcate the several issues associated with Lessing's famous image, and to do so in a way that clarifies the general problem of Christian theology's relation to history and historical inquiry. What this strategy sacrifices in the way of both historical richness and theological construction will, I trust, be offset by the clarification and refinement of some familiar but difficult conceptual matters.

Chapters 2 and 3, then, are devoted to a careful examination of Lessing's own discussion of the ditch. The main burden of these chapters will be to locate those numerous and peculiar instances of cross-threading that Lessing manages to pack into so small a space. Chapters 4 and 5, in turn, consist of a sustained inquiry into the response to the ditch offered in Kierkegaard's *Philosophical Fragments* and *Concluding Unscientific Postscript*. Although Kierkegaard is, for the most part, far more clear-headed and consistent than Lessing in his treatment of these matters, his legacy to twentieth-century discussions of faith and history remains perverse as well as profound. In particular, Kierkegaard's characterization of historical knowledge as "approximation knowledge" perpetuates a mistaken yet influential view of Kierkegaard's own reasons for insulating faith from historical inquiry. There is indeed a Kierkegaardian impasse between Christian faith and historical knowledge; but, as I hope to show in these chapters, this impasse does not arise because historical knowledge is merely approximate.

Although the present inquiry is not intended to be an effort in theological construction, the informed reader will, along the way, doubtless grasp certain implications for contemporary efforts to address the issue of theology's relation to history and historical research. The purpose of chapters 6 and 7 is to make some of these implications explicit.

In the conviction that we stand to learn more from specific case studies than from sweeping generalizations, I have elected to discuss more recent problems concerning theology and history in terms of some fairly specific examples. The inquiry up to that point will suggest three issues in particular that are worth examining in their more contemporary settings: the problem of theology's relationship to the presuppositions of historical inquiry; the question of relating Christian truth claims to universal metaphysical truths that are logically independent of the occurrence of any particular historical event; and the intimate relationship in our time between strategies for eliminating historical-critical problems and invocations of the fundamentally Kantian dualism between fact and value. Perhaps predictably, the first issue will be investigated through reference to Ernst Troeltsch, the second through consideration of a debate associated with Bultmann, and the third through an examination of Wolfhart Pannenberg's suspicion of Kantian tendencies in modern Protestant theology.

When brought to bear on these more recent thinkers and their dialogue partners, the light previously shed on Lessing's image of the ugly ditch will, I think, illuminate the category mistakes we continue to make in discussions of theology and history. We are, in other words, heirs of Lessing in several different senses, not all of them flattering. The frequently unheeded moral that applies to Lessing and Kierkegaard applies, I think, to more recent theologians as well: by the time they get around to characterizing historical knowledge, all the important things have already been decided. If this is true, then to address the general problems of theology and history as though historiographical difficulties are determinative would be, in some sense at least, to miss the point.

2

The Accidental Truths of History and the Necessary Truths of Reason

Indeed, doesn't it seem obvious that the possibility of a language-game is conditioned by certain facts?
—*Ludwig Wittgenstein,* On Certainty

THE ACCIDENTAL TRUTHS OF HISTORY

As its title suggests, Lessing's "On the Proof of the Spirit and of Power" deals with the problem of proving the truth of Christianity, particularly through historical means. In an important sense, then, some of the difficulties that gradually force Lessing to speak of a ditch would fail to materialize at all if we were simply to deny at the outset that Christianity were the sort of thing calling for "proof." It is not really the issue of proof, however, that underlies the influence Lessing's discussion would have on subsequent religious thought. Instead, it is the subtle, if occasionally misleading, manner in which he explores the bearing that a past event can have on a present-day faith.

Lessing begins by facing the problem introduced by our temporal distance from religiously momentous events of the past. By distinguishing between miracles and fulfilled prophecies "which I myself experience," and those "of which I only know from history that others say they have experienced them," Lessing poses the obvious difficulty of tying religious conviction to historical reports.[1] "If I had lived at the time of Christ," he tells us, "then of course the prophecies fulfilled in his person would have made me pay great attention to him." If "I had actually seen him do miracles," Lessing goes on, "I would have believed him in all things in which equally indisputable experiences did not tell against him."[2]

But Lessing does not live at the time of Christ, when miracles and fulfilled prophecies constituted the "proof of the spirit and of power." He lives instead in an age when the "proof of the spirit and of power no longer has any spirit or power, but has sunk to the level

of human testimonies of spirit and power."[3] This comment clearly
signals a suspicion about replacing firsthand experience with reports about someone else's experience, a suspicion fueled, presumably, by concerns about the reliability of such reports. Lessing ampli-
fies his point with an observation that, in various versions, would be
made by numerous succeeding religious thinkers. In Lessing's
words, "all historical certainty is much too weak to replace this
apparent proof of the proof which has lapsed." For

> how is it to be expected of me that the same inconceivable truths
> which sixteen to eighteen hundred years ago people believed on the
> strongest inducement should be believed by me to be equally valid on
> an infinitely lesser inducement? Or is it invariably the case, that what I
> read in reputable historians is just as certain for me as what I myself
> experience? I do not know that anyone has ever asserted this.[4]

The "inconceivable truths" here concern the status of Jesus as
savior and Son of God, while the "strongest inducement" to believing such truths is the firsthand experience of miracles and fulfilled
prophecies which serve to confirm the appropriateness of these
christological titles. In these comments we have a classic statement
of the ugly ditch in its temporal aspect. The confession of faith refers
to certain historical events, and those events—particularly the Old
Testament prophecies fulfilled in the coming of Jesus, and the miracles performed by him authenticating his status—are crucial for
human salvation. However, if I do not have immediate, firsthand
experience of the events in question, but only the testimony of
others, then I must always contend with a degree of doubt concerning their occurrence, no matter how trustworthy the testimony may
seem to be. This difficulty becomes even more burdensome if it
turns out that such testimony as I do have is not even from the
eyewitnesses themselves, but is the second- or thirdhand reporting
of the original testimony.

Now, reliance on the experience, testimony, and authority of others
is not an uncommon occurrence in everyday life. And, in principle at
least, the same element of doubt that Lessing is referring to in this
religious context attends these more commonplace instances of relying on the authority of others in the fashioning of our beliefs about the
world. In everyday life, in other words, the lingering residue of doubt is
typically ignored. In religious matters, however, that which is being
reported is incomparably momentous, and even the slightest bit of
doubt is therefore extremely alarming, undermining the trust and

assurance of any believer aware of the problem. Only firsthand, personal experience, it seems, satisfies the conditions required to believe the "inconceivable truths" in question.

All of Lessing's comments at this early stage in his essay signal a fundamentally empiricist cast of mind. Immediate experience is the epistemological yardstick over against which all other forms of knowledge and certainty are measured. Firsthand sense experience of observable events is the contrast case informing the criticism of all historical certainty as "weak"; from a rigidly empiricist standpoint, the "past-ness" of historical events poses epistemological difficulties of a uniquely pressing sort. Even the belief and trust in Jesus that would be provided by immediate experience of his miracles can be potentially subverted by other, "equally indisputable experiences" that "tell against him." Firsthand, unmediated experience alone appears to offer the sort of "proof" in religious matters that will banish unbelief and settle our skepticism. Accounts of theological problems due to temporal distance and difficulties of historical reconstruction often have this same empiricist criterion as the implicit gauge of historical certainty.

Moreover, difficulties of assent and conviction are further compounded in Lessing's discussion by the peculiar nature of the events in question. Problems of temporal distance and reliance on testimony merge together with questions of probability and natural law, and Lessing's manner of dealing with this confluence of issues virtually assures a losing situation for the person who is not an eyewitness. This is because he takes one type of historical evidence for the miraculous events in question—the testimony of the apostles and saints—and implicitly subordinates it to a second type of historical evidence—his contemporary understanding of what things are physically impossible or highly improbable. This second type of evidence is not so much an independent source of information as it is a corrective to other, more informative types of historical evidence.[5] Lessing deploys this corrective in a way that eliminates the possibility of accepting miracle reports as historically reliable, the trustworthiness of those testifying notwithstanding. For the wedge he has driven between religious conviction based upon eyewitness experience, and conviction based upon evidence provided in the form of human testimony, yields the further difference between "miracles before my own eyes [that] are immediate in their effect" and miracles that "have to work through a medium which takes away all their force."[6] Within the terms laid down by Lessing's essay, the "force" provided by the miracles can only be replaced by new miracles that would then constitute the proof of the original proof. And, says Lessing in a comment that is surely ironic, "I live in the eighteenth century, in which miracles no longer happen."[7]

Much like Hume, then, Lessing is exploring the connection between miracle and testimony from the standpoint of the principle of analogy. That is, before I can even consider accepting reports of putatively historical events as true, I must be able to cite analogous events in my own present-day experience.[8] Experiencing analogous events is by no means a sufficient condition for accepting the historical reports put before me, but for Lessing as for Hume, it is apparently a necessary condition. Even the testimony of such exemplary witnesses as apostles and saints is insufficient to offset the need for a contemporary analogue: the corrective role played by my own experience of how things go in the world is more decisive than even the most compelling testimony coming from the most trustworthy witnesses. The issue of authority in religious matters is here tilted decisively in an empiricist direction. Consequently, when the historical events in question involve apparent violations of natural law, the principle of analogy effectively enforces a permanent skepticism, over against which sheer credulity is the only solution. The result is a powerful case against an assured and unproblematic belief "at second hand," and a fundamental disadvantage increasingly accruing to later generations of potential believers. The proof of the spirit and of power has indeed "sunk" to the level of human testimonies, and the damage to religion threatens the chief supports undergirding the modern-day believer.

The obviously empiricist tone of Lessing's discussion of temporal distance thereby suggests that his chief concern is with strictly *factual* questions. Whether or not certain events actually occurred is the cardinal theme running through this portion of his essay. Moreover, the standard for the ideal warrants for assessing this factual issue is an uncomplicated empiricist one. Lessing never even hints that firsthand experience itself suffers from any epistemological difficulties that might lead us to question *it;* believing one's own eyes and ears appears to be a straightforward and unproblematic procedure. Instead, all of the emphasis is on the difficulties that begin to develop as soon as an event is "historical" and people are left to wonder: "Did it really happen?" Those who actually witnessed the event really *know* the anser to this question. Those who are not eyewitnesses may have strong opinions on the matter and may even feel certain about what the historical facts are, depending on their attitudes toward the original witnesses, the tradition about the witnesses, and the events themselves. But they can never really *know* the answer to the factual question. It is just here, then, with the adjudication of the factual issue, that the specific problem of historical knowledge and historical reconstruction resides. The difficulties with historical knowledge are illuminated through contrast with the unproblematic knowledge enjoyed by the eyewitness.

All of this seems clear and straightforward, somewhat dated, and perhaps even a bit banal. It is crucial, however, to notice that Lessing has in fact cross-threaded two very different issues here, and he has done so in a way that assures serious confusion later in his essay. For there is, first, the empiricist assumption that immediate, firsthand experience is uniquely trustworthy and the ideal basis for religious belief that puts historical knowledge into question; but, second, there is the much more subtle assumption that the truth of Christianity is automatically confirmed by the occurrence of a certain sort of event. These two assumptions are not merely different; they are different in important ways. And, when considering the issue of temporal distance, Lessing simply ignores the serious problem of inference plaguing the second assumption, apparently taking for granted the prevailing eighteenth-century view that a miracle or fulfilled prophecy is the appropriate and unambiguous evidence for the truth of Christianity.[9] He assumes, in other words, that certain types of historical events—miracles and fulfilled prophecies—convey their religious meaning univocally and without the possibility of conflicting interpretations. From this standpoint, the major question naturally becomes the sheer likelihood that a certain sort of event occurred, the religious meaning of which is presumably self-evident.

The peculiarity of this is that Lessing himself goes on to wonder aloud how we can effect precisely *this* transition from historical event to religious truth. We see here the important shift that Lessing makes from temporal to metaphysical problems. He does not announce the shift but simply executes it, and the resulting confusions are no doubt closely related to the indirect and nonconfessional way in which Lessing typically enters into religious debates. As we have seen, Lessing has initially distinguished between miracles "that occur before my eyes" that "are immediate in their effect," and miracles that "have to work through a medium which takes away all their force." He is clearly indicating here that the inferential route from experienced event to religious conclusion is far less problematic than the corresponding route from historical reports to belief in the events reported. In other words, the linkage between miraculous event and religious truth is made to appear uncomplicated: the issue of what constitutes sufficient evidence for the proof of a religious claim is apparently settled; only the likelihood of the events in question remains in dispute.

Lessing, however, will later put into question the very inferential process he appears here to be taking for granted. How, he asks, can we be expected to "jump with a historical truth to a quite different class of truths" and demand of ourselves that we should form all of our "metaphysical and moral ideas accordingly."[10] He continues: "If on historical grounds I have no objection to the statement that this Christ himself rose from the dead, must I therefore accept it as true that this risen Christ was the Son of God?"[11] What was simply assumed without question when the temporal ditch was at stake gradually becomes the very point under debate in Lessing's essay.

Thus, the factual issue is displaced by the problem of successfully relating two different classes of truths, the historical and the religious. *This* problem threatens the eyewitness every bit as much as it haunts the person who did not see firsthand, which means that successful resolution does not depend on accurate historical reconstruction. The epistemological ideal that historical reconstruction attempts to approximate is eyewitness experience, the aim being to give us access to what the "facts" are. Even if we know what the relevant historical facts are, however, we still face the difficulty of jumping from one truth to a "quite different class of truths." Moreover, we come up against the serious difficulty of correctly interpreting even such facts as we may all agree upon. As the temporal problem is superseded by these new problems, and the factual issue loses its position of dominance, anxieties about historical reports and historical reconstruction become less and less urgent. Our final estimate of the degree to which accurate historical research is a true problem for religion will depend largely upon how the metaphysical issue concerning different classes of truths is ultimately resolved. In Lessing's case, it will be resolved through a fundamentally rationalist conception of religious truth, meaning that authentic religious belief will in no way be dependent upon assessing historical reports and achieving an accurate picture of the past. The problem of temporal distance turns out to be not at all a problem for Lessing.

CONTINGENCY, NECESSITY, AND RELIGIOUS TRUTH

As Lessing further considers the relation between historical truths and religious belief, he argues that "historical truths cannot be demonstrated."[12] He has in mind here "to demonstrate" in the deductive, logical sense, thereby betraying for the first time his commitment to dividing truth claims according to their logical status and not simply according to their relationship to present experience. The comparison of historical truth and logical demonstration is the occasion for Lessing's introduction of the distinction between contingent and necessary truths. Lessing borrows this distinction from Leibniz, whose philosophy, like that of Spinoza, greatly influenced him.[13] For Lessing as for Leibniz, a proposition is necessarily true if its negation is self-contradictory; but if we can, without contradiction, think the negation or denial of a proposition, then it is not necessarily true but is true (if at all) only contingently. The proposition merely "happens" to be true.

When Lessing says that "no historical truth can be demonstrated," it is not clear if he has in mind historical events or historical knowledge. Nor is this clear in his famous comment that "accidental truths of history can never become the proof of necessary truths of reason."[14] But the weight of the entire essay seems to fall on the epistemological issue, particularly when Lessing refers to certain reports as being "as reliable as historical truths ever can be," or when he says that it "is not more than historically certain" that Jesus spoke certain words.[15]

What is clear is that Lessing's attention has shifted away from the problem of temporal distance. Historical truths, in whatever sense, are now set in relation to the apodictic certainties of logic, and not to the presumed assurances of firsthand experience. A new, nontemporal ditch is coming into view. Obviously, no historical truth can ever be "demonstrated" in the sense conveyed by deductive logic, since the events in the past concerning which we develop empirical claims, and the claims themselves, did not have to occur or develop, but might have been otherwise. This is the whole point of contingency.

As Lessing shifts away from the temporal-factual issue, his discussion assumes a new richness and develops a more significant relationship to ongoing problems in Christian theology: he is implicitly moving from a consideration of matters of fact to an exploration of the problem of reason and revelation. Moreover, by framing the issue in terms dictated by an examination of historical truth from the standpoint of philosophical necessity, Lessing is anticipating issues that would remain central to German religious thought during the important decades ahead—the problem of grasping the relationship between rational necessity and historical particularity, and then relating *this* issue to the traditional question of historical revelation, would be of major concern to Kant, Hegel, and their numerous lesser followers. Furthermore, Hegel's inversion of Lessing's definition of the issue, through his fusing of the historical and the necessary, would shape in decisive ways Kierkegaard's eventual commentary on the ditch and its problems. For one of Kierkegaard's chief reasons for considering the ditch at all would be to discredit Hegel's importation of necessity into the historical realm, since, for Kierkegaard, only if we appreciate the full contingency of history do we truly grasp the meaning of divine grace and the dialectics of Christian existence. The contrast between contingency and necessity is crucial for thinking through this axial Kierkegaardian claim.

In the case of Lessing's "On the Proof of the Spirit and of Power," the appearance of the notion of necessity marks the transition from temporal to metaphysical concerns.[16] Prior to this point, as we have seen, Lessing has contrasted knowledge gained from historical reports with knowledge gained from personal experience, thereby conveying serious misgivings about the reliability of historical reports, together with an apparent confidence in both the trustworthiness and the religious significance of firsthand experience. Now, however, he is explaining his remark that "reports which we have of these prophecies and miracles are as reliable as historical truths can be" by claiming that "historical truths cannot be demonstrated" in the deductive, Leibnizian sense.[17] In other words, he is introducing the quite new argument that historical reports can never be absolutely reliable, *not* because of the absence of firsthand experience or of a present-day analogue, but because historical truths cannot be logically demonstrated. This point might sit there dumbly were it not for the fact that Lessing goes on to exploit it from the standpoint of his implicit commitment regarding the rational nature of religious truth. He may, as commentators are fond of saying, have one foot in nineteenth-century romanticism, but in most respects Lessing is still an Enlightenment rationalist.

Consequently, the reason that the relationship between history and necessary truth is a problem at all for Lessing is that he approaches it with the view that authentic religious claims are more like logical truths, known a priori to be necessarily the case, than they are like contingent empirical truths. This conviction on his part, together with his more explicit attention devoted to logical detail, guarantees the appearance of the ugly ditch in its most familiar form: the ditch between the accidental truths of history and the necessary truths of reason. As the true dimensions of this ditch become clear, we see that the purely temporal issue with which Lessing begins his essay is simply beside the point. What began as a factual problem is abruptly transformed into a problem that cannot be resolved through adjudicating matters of fact. Lessing the empiricist has become Lessing the rationalist.

We have, then, a logical lesson regarding the unnecessary or contingent character of the truths conveyed by historical reports. In accordance with his primary emphasis on the notion of proof, Lessing applies this logical lesson to the problem of proving something through historical means. Here he exposes the obvious fallacy involved in moving from historical data to the proof of a necessary truth of reason, and it is at this point that he offers us his famous formula: "If no historical truth can be demonstrated, then nothing can be demonstrated by means of historical truths. That is: accidental truths of history can never become the proof of necessary truths of reason."[18] The point, of course, involves the illegitimacy of ever employing a claim about the past as part of an argument aimed at arriving at a conclusion that is true by necessity; after all, such a conclusion would always be undermined by the contingent, empirical character of the historical claim serving as one of the premises of the argument. Much of the subsequent influence of Lessing's essay is due to the way it pursues the religious implications of this truism.

It is important to pause momentarily to emphasize what sort of ditch Lessing is now offering us and to clarify the religious commitments one would need to have to be anxious about it. Lessing has set aside his original temporal ditch and replaced it with a ditch between the accidental truths of history and the necessary truths of reason. His problem is that of effecting a transition from the one side of the ditch to the other, if historical truths never admit of logical demonstration.

Now the important thing to notice is that there is a religious problem here only if one holds that religious truths are necessary and not contingent: contingency is nerve-wracking only for those who have a stake in necessity. Thus, Lessing is implicitly revealing that authentic religion takes its lifeblood from the universal, rational truths it expresses, and not from the unique and particular— that is to say, contingent—events of history. As a virtual monist, due no doubt to the influence on him of Spinoza, Lessing really has no wish to construe true religion in terms of the positivity entailed by the orthodox conception of historical revelation.[19] This means that truth in religious matters will not hang on the occurrence or nonoccurrence of specific historical events. The meaning, as distinct from the truth, of authentic religion may come to expression in historical events, and this is largely the point of Lessing's fresh conception of the intimate and still important relationship between history and religion developed in his "Education of the Human Race." Yet, as he says even in that context, historical revelation "gives nothing to the human race which human reason could not arrive at on its own."[20]

Lessing's exploration of the contingency-necessity distinction is thus his way of mediating the divergent claims of experience and reason in our religious life. His total approach to this difficult problem is far more nuanced than much competing Enlightenment religious thought, and doing full justice to it would take us well beyond a consideration of his image of the ditch.[21] However, as Henry Allison has forcefully argued, the most distinctive result of his approach to the problem of relating history, revelation, and reason is the way Lessing divorces the question of the *truth* of Christianity from the question of the *facticity* of historical revelation: Christianity is true, not because of certain public, factual, and altogether accidental historical idiosyncracies that set it off from our rationality, but because of its rational "inner truth" that is binding even on the will of God.[22]

This is the standpoint informing Lessing's famous comment that "religion is not true because the evangelists and apostles taught it; but they taught it because it is true."[23] Again, Lessing betrays here his unwillingness to base true religion on any particular historical event, and his need to seek out the rational, "necessary" meaning of what comes to expression in history and even in christology. In this, he is not merely eliminating the category of miraculous intervention from the religious scene, but he is cutting the knot between religious truth and any particular historical event understood purely as "event." The religious significance of history does not reside here. Instead, as he tells us in his "Education of the Human Race," historical events bear religious significance in their capacity as a kind of "primer" or as the "clothing and style" of truths that would otherwise remain abstract and perhaps even unknown—but nonetheless true.[24] Its being known is not a necessary property of a true religious claim.

Lessing's position thus suggests that history is, to be sure, religiously important, but in a fundamentally epistemological, and not ontological, sense. The word here for "education" is *Erziehung*, which has strong connotations of a fashioning, shaping, or cultivating, over time, of something like "character"—a process that cannot occur quickly (like cramming for a test based on memorization) but requires a significant temporal span for its full realization (as is presumably involved in the acquisition of profound insight or wis-

dom). True religion does indeed benefit from history. Even so, religious truths are not true because certain events happen. It is history's pedagogical capacity, and not the brute ontological fact or
"eventful" character of any particular occurrence, that is crucial for
Lessing.

Because of Lessing's attempts to take history—or at least historical development—seriously, his position appears somewhat un-
stable or perhaps merely tentative. Such a result, of course, hardly
distinguishes this aspect of his religious thought from most other
aspects. With this thinker, a truly systematic account of a complex
conceptual issue would not be in character.

To Lessing's credit, however, his way of posing the historical issue
would remain standard during the creative decades ahead. Indeed,
much of the history of the philosophy of religion between Lessing
and Kierkegaard could be written in terms of the role played by the
contingency-necessity distinction. The peculiar junction of difficult
issues is made more complex by the fact that, not only can we take
historical truth in two different senses (as event or as knowledge
claim), but the very category of necessity involves a corresponding
ambiguity: it can be a purely logical category, bearing on the nature
of propositions; or it can be given ontological weight, and bear on
the nature of events themselves.

Kant, for example, would emphasize the former, or logical, sense
of necessity. In terms of religious matters, this emphasis is made
particularly clear in Kant's efforts, in *Religion Within the Limits of
Reason Alone*, to ferret out the rational religious kernel lurking
within the contingent husk of revealed religion. In this work, Kant
clearly takes revealed or historical religion seriously, but only insofar as it can be understood as the "vehicle" for a pure moral faith.[25]
The parallel with a work like Lessing's "Education of the Human
Race" is readily apparent. Like Lessing, but in a far more systematic form, Kant seeks out necessarily true religious claims, their
truth being logically independent of the occurence of this or that
historical event. The application of his moral hermeneutics to revealed religion thus takes contingent, historical claims as the point
of departure for discovering necessary, rational truth claims. As in
the case of his *Critique of Pure Reason*, Kant's religious writings are
thereby aimed at disclosing and justifying a kind of necessity that
comes to expression in a type of proposition—namely, a synthetic
proposition that can be known a priori. In this setting, history is
important only to the extent that it can trigger or induce awareness
of these synthetic a priori truths, and not because there is a mate-

rial, metaphysical connection between these truths and specific historical events.

In contrast to Kant, Hegel would construe the ontology of history itself in terms of necessity. Depending upon how one interprets Lessing's "Education of the Human Race," Hegel's position, like Kant's, can be viewed as the refinement of a theme already present in veiled form in Lessing. Mediating the contingency-necessity distinction at Kant's merely propositional level becomes, for Hegel, a kind of schoolbook exercise on the way to a higher state of philosophical consciousness.[26] For Hegel, the locus of necessity's most important expression is not Kant's propositional realm, but the historical realm itself. Here, logic will continue to be important, as it was for Kant; but it will be a logic with a dialectical difference, disclosed within history itself. In the framework of this Hegelian view of history, previous conceptions of historical contingency and particularity are thus fundamentally transformed and, as a consequence, reflection on the topic of historical revelation is revolutionized.[27] Kant, in his endorsement of a moral teleology in his account of history and religion, shows some indications of this more ambitious Hegelian pattern,[28] but he could never find an acceptable route around his own epistemological strictures, laid down in the *Critique of Pure Reason.* Hegel would have no such scruples; he would, in fact, deride philosophers who, like Kant, gave so much prominence to epistemology and who thereby set such rigid boundaries to their freedom of philosophical movement.

The concept of necessity would thus be philosophically engrossing for both Kant and Hegel, but in very different ways. How this difference then factors into religious reflection both illuminates and justifies the common observation that Kant wished to give the old religious forms a new philosophical meaning, while Hegel wanted to give the old religious meanings a new philosophical form.

Problems connected with relating necessity to religious matters are particularly acute with respect to the topic of historical revelation. It would be from the standpoint of rational necessity that traditional Pauline language about the "scandal" or "offense" of Christianity would take on a new meaning during the Enlightenment and afterwards. There is not merely the problem of the contingency, particularity, and potentially miraculous character of historical revelation as traditionally conceived; there is also the scandalous presumption that a unique historical moment actually introduced religious information not available, through natural human capacities, to all persons at all times, resulting, apparently, in the exclusion of countless numbers of people from the possibility of salvation. Such topics had been furiously debated by the deists and others by the time Lessing, Kant, and Hegel arrived on the scene.

Consequently, the debate over revelation would turn largely on whether one understood necessity to be a religious friend or foe. For some, the very notion of a unique historical revelation simply had to be abandoned, since it was not only intellectually repugnant, but a symbol of the obscurantism and authoritarianism of eccelsiastical religion. The issue at stake here, finally, is *positivity*, a term not easily defined but already referred to here as a definite historical revelation or divine intrusion which becomes the source of theological authority. The content of the revelation is retained and propagated, often in propositional form, by an eccelesiastical institution that derives its own authority from the original revelation itself, as preserved in scripture and, perhaps, tradition.[29] In the familiar terms employed in Enlightenment religious debates, a positive religion is revealed, not natural, and typically includes supernaturalist features. Religious truths come to the believer as genuinely informative propositions from the "outside," requiring assent and obedience, guided, if necessary, by the disciplining functions of the ecclesiastical body. Correct belief is of momentous importance. The positivity issue thus suggests yet another way of posing the problem of the ditch: "Do I require for my salvation propositional news that comes to me from the 'outside'? What if this news is strange, odd, or a scandal to my intellect? How do I cross *that* ditch?"

In contrast, a natural, nonpositive religion involves authorities that are internal and personal, rather than external and impersonal. The result is an emphasis on the "inwardness" of authentic faith. Religious truth is always something the believer either already knows or has the natural capacity for understanding; an authentic religious message thereby finds its natural point of contact "within" the believer and does not have to be imposed or forced on the believer from the outside. Correct belief is not as important as sincerity and moral conduct—hypocrisy is worse than unorthodox views. The "religion of the head" is not as crucial as the "religion of the heart."

The locus for thinking through the twin problems of revelation and positivity would be christology. And it is primarily for this reason that the positivity issue is at the center of debates over Lessing's ditch—christology is the link between the problem of positivity and the problem of faith's relation to historical knowledge. The basic options defining Protestant thought since roughly

1750 are readily evident in the responses elicited by this juncture of historical revelation, positivity, and christology: Jesus is required for salvation, precisely in the "eventful" character of his life and career (e.g., Kierkegaard); Jesus is not really required but is nonetheless a particularly vivid reminder or teacher of religious truths that all rational beings are capable of knowing at any time, at least in principle (e.g., Lessing, Kant); Jesus is decidedly not required for true religion or human salvation, and the message about him is either a fraud and a lie, perpetrated to serve the interests of the priestly class (e.g., Reimarus, Nietzsche), or it is simply an intellectual mistake, explainable through reference to the primitive cultural situation of the earliest Christians (e.g., radical historicists).

The difficulties posed to theology by questions of historical method and historical skepticism will vary widely, depending upon which of these positions is adopted. Since representatives of all sides in this debate can and do refer to the contingent or risky character of historical knowledge, it is important to appreciate the different ways this common observation may or may not wreak theological havoc.

Much of what follows in this and the succeeding chapters will be an attempt to further differentiate Lessing and Kierkegaard on this cluster of issues. My aim in this is not merely to illuminate two important thinkers, but to demarcate two quite different models for reflection on revelation, christology, and faith. In a broad sense, these two models—Lessing's rationalist one and Kierkegaard's existentialist one—remain clearly evident in more recent Protestant thought, however much the original rationalism and existentialism of these two thinkers have been refined or eclipsed. The most important issues demarcating these christological positions are: (1) the degree to which historical revelation is theologically decisive as "event" and not merely as an "illustration" of general truths, and (2) the degree to which natural human capacities, or anthropological givens, play the defining role in our apprehension of the point or meaning of revelation. The question is whether we generate a christology by *conferring* on Jesus a certain status—illustrative, symbolic, "mythological"—the nature and point of which are determined through prior appeal to universal canons of truth; or whether, alternatively, we generate a christology through inquiring into what is *unique* to Jesus as a particular historical figure, whose very existence is decisive for salvation. Lessing represents the first position and Kierkegaard, the second.

ELIMINATING THE HISTORICAL PROBLEM

The preceding discussion brings into even bolder relief the artificiality of Lessing's starting point in "On the Proof of the Spirit and of Power." If religion draws its lifeblood from a rational inner truth, rather than from a specific historical revelation that is decisive in its "eventful" character, then there is no need to invest the gap between the eyewitness and the noneyewitness with decisive religious significance. At the most, such a gap could have only epistemological significance, insofar as witnessing a revelation might—to use Kierkegaard's expression—serve as the "occasion" on which I become explicitly conscious of a truth I already implicitly know.

In this tension between two different types of ditches, we once again confront the troublesome equivocation running throughout Lessing's essay between the historical as a kind of event and the historical as a kind of knowledge claim. The event aspect relates to the positivity issue, and on this Lessing has established a position that requires no particular event for there to be such a thing as religious truth. The knowledge aspect, on the other hand, involves the epistemological difficulties connected with historical reports, which, as we have seen, is finally a concern about what the "facts" of history are. But it is obvious that Lessing's position on the positivity or event issue supersedes these epistemological worries. For if religious truth is not dependent upon the occurrence of any particular event, then religious faith does not hang on matters of fact. If this is so, then faith must not depend upon the results of historical research. When the issue is posed in terms of contingency and necessity, the problem is not the likelihood of certain reported events; rather, it is the clash between two different classes of truth.

Moreover, this set of considerations bears heavily on the problem of inference shadowing the connection between even firsthand experience and religious conclusion. After all, Lessing's complaint that the accidental truths of history can never prove the necessary truths of reason undercuts not only the religious value of historical testimony but that of firsthand experience as well, a point that lies buried in Lessing's essay because of the way he has, without warning, switched the issues on us. To be sure, testimonies cannot replace firsthand experience; but not even firsthand experience can yield a necessary truth of reason.[30] In contrast to the temporal ditch Lessing offers us at the outset, his new, metaphysical ditch offers no real advantage to the eyewitness to historical revelation. That Lessing himself suddenly directs his discussion away from the issue of firsthand experience reflects his underlying commitment to the necessary, nonempirical character of religious truth. It comes as no surprise, then, that he ends his essay with an analogy drawn from the world of mathematics, the point of which is to consider truths that are and always have been true regardless of how and when they were actually recognized.[31] This very illustration, however, reflects just how far Lessing's essay has strayed from its starting point.

We can see, then, that there are at least three different strands woven into the fabric of Lessing's discussion: the basically Humean point, arising out of the problem of temporal distance, concerning the value of historical reports or testimony; the distinction between contingent historical truths and the necessary truths of reason, resulting in a metaphysical instead of a merely temporal problem; and the underlying commitment on Lessing's part to the rational, necessary character of authentic religious claims. This third point is a function of Lessing's rejection of positivity as a religious requirement, and it affects the resolution of the other two points in significant ways. For, as we have just seen, Lessing does not really have to worry about the factual difficulties conveyed by the temporal problem, and this in turn means that he does not need to worry about bridging the ditch between the contingent truths of history and the necessary truths of reason. For Lessing already has a secure foothold on the necessity side, and all he really needs to do is to find a suitable auxiliary role for history to play in religious matters, which is what he tentatively achieves through the scheme of divine education in his "Education of the Human Race."

The point, then, is that Lessing does not have to leap the specific ditch for which his essay is most famous. By virtue of his essentially rationalist posture concerning the positivity issue, he is in effect rejecting the notion that the truth of authentic religion is dependent upon the occurrence of certain historical events or on the emergence at an identifiable moment in time of a truth not previously available to us.[32] The "eventful" character of putative historical revelations is not crucial for his position. The *meaning* of Christianity may well be illuminated both through reference to the past and by virtue of the sheer process of historical development; however, this is quite a different matter from the question of the *truth* of Christianity. To draw on history to illuminate the meaning of Christianity or to trigger the discovery of its truth—but not actually to underwrite its truth—will not require for its successful execution the actual occurrence of the events in question. Instead, drawing on history in this way simply requires that the events referred to successfully illuminate or illustrate a truth that is logically independent of their occurrence and which can, in principle at least, be determined apart from reference to them. Without the sheer process of history we might not discover religious truth in *fact;* but this is only to say that the process of history is potentially decisive in a pedagogical, and not an ontological, sense.

Consequently, on this view we could agree that certain religiously significant historical events are purely legendary or mythical in character and suffer no theological loss, as long as the appropriate religious apprehension or moment of religious insight were triggered by reference to those events. What is crucial in achieving *this* insight is not the actual occurrence of the specified events, but the deployment of a hermeneutical principle that offers us access to the religious truth latent in the putatively historical report. In other words, calling a supposedly historical event legendary or mythical is not a rejection of its religious significance; rather, it is an invitation to seek out the "real," nonhistorical meaning of the event. To seek out such a meaning, one already has to have in mind a theory of what makes religion true, if not the actual occurrence of certain historical events. For all the nuances attending his position— introduced especially by his "Education of the Human Race"—Lessing is finally saying that authentic religion is true because it is rational, and this commitment implicitly shapes his treatment of the historical problem, guaranteeing the formulation of a ditch in terms of contingency and necessity.

Ultimately, then, Lessing's position on faith and historical knowledge is derived from more fundamental commitments concerning faith and reason on the one hand, and reason and revelation on the other: authentic faith is rational and potentially universalizable, meaning that it does not hang on the acceptance of any historical facts; and historical revelations do not introduce new and indispensable religious information but simply illustrate, or bring into our field of vision, what we are capable of knowing all along.

The implications of this general position for the specific question of faith's relation to historical research are glaringly obvious and have already been alluded to. Authentic religious faith is simply not dependent upon any form of factual or empirical inquiry, historical or otherwise. This result is the natural function of Lessing's rejection of the dependence of true religion upon the occurrence of any particular historical event: clearly, if religious claims are not dependent for their truth upon reference to any particular event, they can hardly be dependent upon the results of historical inquiry. Whatever the confusions in Lessing's essay, the dominant and controlling role is played, not by historical skepticism, but by the underlying position on reason and revelation. For Lessing, truth in religious matters points to something necessarily the case. However balanced his employment of necessity would become in his efforts still to take history seriously, this concept would nonetheless serve him as the touchstone of true religion and would underwrite his formulation of the ditch in its most familiar form. And, as soon as a commitment to the necessary character of authentic religion is made, the tie between salvation and any particular historical event is cut. Even less, then, is there a binding tie between faith and historical research.

Lessing's position thereby has the effect of insulating Christian faith from even the most destructive consequences of historical research. The results of such research may be theoretically interesting, but they can never be theologically germane; there is no point where negative historical results can gain purchase on questions of religious truth. The necessary character of authentic religious truth leaves history with, at most, a pedagogical role to play—which, to be sure, may be a very considerable role indeed. Even so, any clash between "the historian and the believer" of the sort that would haunt other modern religious thinkers simply never comes into view: with no theological need to *confirm* any particular historical datum, there is nothing to fear in the possibility of the *disconfirmation* of events reported by the tradition.

Still, not even Lessing is off the hook yet, for there are other problems lurking in his essay. Once again, without warning Lessing executes an important shift in his consideration of the metaphysical ditch by substituting christological assertions for what he sometimes calls necessary truths of reason. And even he appears to grasp that christological claims are not rationally, necessarily true. In effect, Lessing has introduced a new version of his metaphysical ditch between two classes of truths: it now involves the gap between contingent, historical truths and dogmatic christological claims of a presumably universal import. This ditch will be of far more interest to Lessing's post-Enlightenment audience, since it is precisely the problem involved in all efforts to relate the Jesus of history to faith and theology. Moreover, as Lessing's own treatment of this new issue suggests, this gap between history and dogmatics is closely related to the "existential ditch" involved in the process of religious appropriation.

It is time, then, to see what Lessing has to say about this new assortment of difficulties.

History, Dogmatics, and Religious Appropriation

They base enormous things on this evidence.
—Ludwig Wittgenstein, "Lectures on Religious Belief"

HISTORICAL EVENT AND DOGMATIC CLAIM

The discussion in the previous chapter unveiled two different ditches present in Lessing's "On the Proof of the Spirit and of Power." First, there is the temporal ditch interposed between the present-day believer and revelatory historical events, and second, there is a metaphysical ditch involving the disjunction between historical and religious truths. We have seen that Lessing's way of approaching the second difficulty both supersedes and neutralizes the problems intrinsic to the first issue. However much Lessing may talk about historical reports and the risks involved in relying upon them, it turns out that his own religious position remains untouched by considerations of historical fact.

We have also seen that Lessing poses the second, or metaphysical, divide in terms suggested by the distinction between contingency and necessity. It is this distinction that shapes Lessing's ditch in the manner that is most familiar to us. As I have indicated, the latent rationalism running through Lessing's essay, with its implicit rejection of positivity and its endorsement of universal natural religion, suggests the firm footing that Lessing himself has on the necessity side of this ditch. There is a strong element of the devil's advocate in the plaintive tone characterizing Lessing's discussion of religion and history, a not uncommon tendency in his treatment of religious matters.

The issue, however, does not rest here, as though Lessing were content to embrace a shallow deism. Instead, he goes on to probe the metaphysical ditch in a manner that continues to be of considerable interest and relevance, lifting his essay out of the parochialism characteristic of much Enlightenment religious thought. For in what is in effect a confusion on his part, Lessing introduces examples of religious truths, to be drawn from historical events, that are *not* necessary truths. Instead, they are christological claims. In what is perhaps the richest part of his essay, Lessing explores the problem of fashioning christological truths from claims about the past, even those claims to which we readily assent. The accent, in other words, is not on the risks of historical reconstruction and the accurate adjudication of matters of fact, nor is it on reconciling the accidental truths of history with philosophical necessity. The accent is instead on successfully relating accidental truths of history to universal truths of a non-necessary sort, represented by orthodox christological claims. It is not the problem of contingency and necessity, but the problem of the historical Jesus and the Christ of faith.

Consequently, whereas Lessing first offered us his metaphysical difficulty in its logical aspect, he now offers the same difficulty with a christological twist. He is in effect bracketing the problem of historical skepticism and now asking what it is that the theologian, *qua* theologian, can possibly do with historical results. Lessing's way of probing this issue anticipates the growing divide between historical research and Christian dogmatics that has been a central feature of the history of Protestant theology during the last two centuries.

> If on historical grounds I have no objection to the statement that Christ raised to life a dead man; must I therefore accept it as true that God has a Son who is of the same essence as himself? What is the connection between my inability to raise any significant objection to the evidence of the former and my obligation to believe something against which my reason rebels? If on historical grounds I have no objection to the statement that this Christ himself rose from the dead, must I therefore accept it as true that this risen Christ was the Son of God?[1]

The essential issue here is the apparent requirement that we "jump with that historical truth to a quite different class of truths," and, says Lessing, "if that is not a metabasis eis allo genos, then I do not know what Aristotle meant by this phrase."[2] As I indicated briefly in the previous chapter, the very point at issue here is the connection between historical event and religious truth that appeared to be no problem at all for Lessing when, at the start of his essay, he posed the temporal-factual difficulty.

Much of the shift in emphasis in Lessing's discussion is due to the nagging equivocation concerning the term *history* that we confront everywhere in his essay. When Lessing poses the ditch in terms of temporal-factual issues, his emphasis is on the historical as a kind of knowledge claim. It is, after all, in terms of historical "reports" that he pursues this aspect of the relation between history and religious faith.

When Lessing poses his ditch in metaphysical terms, however, the accent falls on the historical as a type of event, not as a type of knowledge. This is particularly clear in his statement of the metaphysical problem in its dogmatic-christological form. *Even if* I have no objection on historical grounds to traditional claims about the deeds of Jesus, I am still left wondering what to infer from his ability to calm storms and raise the dead, as well as from his own reported resurrection. Not only is the religious point of these historical events not self-evident, but such religious claims as are traditionally derived from them appear to share no internal, material connection with the original events themselves. "Events" simply do not produce "truths." And to insist that the events related to the appearance of Jesus reveal or disclose just that class of truths associated with orthodox christology is not only to jump from event to truth, but it is to ignore the myriad other "truths" that one could conceivably infer from the events in question. In other words, even assuming that we could fashion a metaphysical bridge between historical event and universal truth claim, there still remains the problem of alternative and conflicting versions of the truths revealed by the events. In principle, the familiarity and sheer staying power of orthodox christological interpretations of the events associated with the historical Jesus do not legitimate those interpretations, over against the possible alternatives.

Just here, as Lessing is investigating the connection between historical event and dogmatic claim, he appears perversely intent on keeping his reader off balance. Instead of sustaining his consideration of the clash between two classes of truths, he reverts to the temporal ditch, implicitly making the problem once again that of firsthand experience over against historical testimony.

> It is said: "The Christ of whom on historical grounds you must allow that he raised the dead, that he himself rose from the dead, said himself that God had a Son of the same essence as himself, and that he is this Son." This would be quite excellent! if only it were not the case that it is not more than historically certain that Christ said this.[3]

Lessing has fallen back here on the factual issue, and, as at the outset of his essay, he implies that the transition from verified fact

to religious conclusion is smooth and uncomplicated—the only com-
plication lies in getting the verification. And, interestingly enough,
it is here, in his reversion to the temporal-factual problem—and *not*
when he compares the accidental truths of history and the necessary
truths of reason—that Lessing says: "That, then, is the ugly, broad
ditch which I cannot get across, however often and however ear-
nestly I have tried to make the leap."[4]

Curiously, then, the context within which Lessing actually employs the image of the ditch suggests that historical certainty is
what is at stake and that the original eyewitness to a historical
revelation is someone to be envied. As we have seen, though, this is
not at all what is at stake in the insight that accidental truths of
history can never become the proof of necessary truths of reason,
which is not a temporal-factual problem. Even less is it what is at
stake in the transition between historical event and dogmatic truth.
These problems, which I have been labeling metaphysical in character, entail genuine incommensurability, requiring for their solution a true leap of the metaphysical imagination, if the two different
sorts of truths are to be coherently integrated. The difficulties posed
here are the sorts of problems that Hegel, more than anyone, would
tackle and attempt to resolve. The problem of temporal distance, on
the other hand, entails no genuine incommensurability but only
permanent nostalgia for someone else's experience.

To put the matter this way is to suggest that, whatever the location in his essay of Lessing's actual reference to a ditch, the temporal-factual problem is not really what is gnawing at him. Clearly his
main point involves the impossibility—in lieu of a dubious metaphysical leap—of reconciling opposing conceptual spheres, whether
we understand the impasse in terms of historical contingency and
philosophical necessity, or in terms of historical contingency and
christological affirmation. By comparison with the difficulties posed
by these dichotomies, the strictly temporal issue seems to be the
least pressing difficulty within Lessing's essay.

An interesting feature of Lessing's essay is his own apparent im-
munity to most of the difficulties broached in it. This is easily
missed because of the plaintive tone of his account of the problems
that history poses for religious conviction. As we have seen, however, the temporal-factual difficulty fades from view once we appreciate Lessing's rationalist conception of religious truth. Furthermore, he does not really need to move from contingent historical
truth to necessary religious truth in a manner requiring their full
integration on the basis of a metaphysical scheme; he simply needs

to show how historical events can illustrate or teach us about truths that are valid independently of any particular historical occurrences. He does not, in other words, need to show us that the truths are true *because* the events took place.

Finally, since Lessing does not embrace an orthodox christology, but thinks of Jesus as primarily a teacher of universal moral truths,[5] he does not have to bridge the gap between the life of Jesus and traditional christological formulations. Lessing's essay graphically reveals how there is indeed a formidable problem here, one that confronts anyone wishing to relate inquiry into the historical Jesus to confessions or affirmations about the Christ. Someone wishing to resolve this difficulty will get no help from Lessing: he perceives the problem and leaves it in place. Unless one is willing to join Lessing in viewing Jesus as mainly a particularly vivid and powerful instance of history teaching us something we could, in principle, have known all along, the impasse between historical event and christological claim—or, alternatively, between historical knowledge and christological claim—remains. Thus, when Lessing discusses the metaphysical difficulty involved in the linkage between history and dogmatics, he is, in effect, simply pinpointing a problem for the reigning orthodoxy of his time and for the ongoing effort to relate the Jesus of history to the Christ of faith. He is not identifying a true problem for those, like himself, who are in the process of transmuting Christian theology into a general philosophy of religion.

It is, after all, Lessing who would go on to write *Nathan the Wise*, that classic Enlightenment statement of religious tolerance that seeks out the one underlying "true" religion residing in each of the world's historical faiths. Lessing would do this by emphasizing simplicity, sincerity, and moral conduct as the chief criteria for truth and authenticity in religious matters.[6] The author of that work is hardly going to be tripped up by orthodox christological difficulties. Indeed, the dramatic form in which Lessing comes the closest to disclosing his own, full religious position perhaps implies a fundamentally aloof or ironic attitude toward "conceptual" difficulties altogether.[7] Profoundly influenced by the Moravians, feeling his way toward a modern theory of aesthetics,[8] and far more nuanced than the deists in his view of history, Lessing is simply not the sort of thinker for whom technical conceptual matters prove to be decisive.

However sympathetically we may sort out Lessing's confusion and interpret his aims, it remains the case that he is offering us more than one ugly ditch and that he is arbitrarily alternating his references to them. To this point, we have confronted: a temporal divide,

separating us from the religiously momentous past, which turns out
to be a basically factual problem; and a metaphysical divide that
comes in two models, one dictated by the philosophical criterion of
necessity and the other by dogmatic christological formulas. Neither of these metaphysical difficulties is eliminated or resolved
through the successful adjudication of matters of fact; this, in turn,
obviously means that neither of them is resolved through successful
historical inquiry. Furthermore, shadowing Lessing's consideration
of these metaphysical issues is the problem of positivity, in the form
already discussed. The issue here is whether or not a specific, identifiable divine intrusion into history, miraculous or not, is required
for religious truth and human salvation. Lessing himself rejects the
need for positive religion, based upon such an intrusion, while he
retains a lively interest in the category of revelation, seeking out the
common ground between what is revealed and what is already implicitly known by us through reason alone. And, elsewhere, Lessing
satisfies what appears to him to be the legitimate claim of history in
religious affairs through the scheme of divine education over time.[9]

There is no doubt a reasonably consistent and cohesive religious
position coming to expression in all of this, despite the purposefully
unsystematic method of its author.[10] The fact remains, however, that
Lessing does not simply leave behind him a degree of puzzlement
concerning his own intentions, but he sows the seeds for considerable confusion when subsequent thinkers refer to "Lessing's ditch" as
though its meaning is self-evident. Are they talking about problems
of historical skepticism and the clash between historiographical and
theological forms of assessment of biblical materials?[11] If so, it
would seem that the temporal-factual issue is at stake, and the chief
question troubling the theologian is: "Did it really happen?" Even
in the absence of full agreement on the "facts," however, this way of
putting the issue implicitly assumes an unproblematic and economical inferential route between established fact and christological claim, something that Lessing—in his clear-headed moments—
recognizes is not unproblematic at all.

Alternatively, when theologians refer to "Lessing's problem" or
"Lessing's ditch," do they have in mind the "scandal of particularity" in the intellectual offense involved in locating truth and salvation in a unique moment of history? If so, the chief difficulty then is
the problem of positivity, and not the problem of historical skepticism and the obstacles coming between us and historical facts. For,
as in Lessing's case, the severity of the problems posed by historiographical difficulties will depend on how the positivity issue is han-

dled; theological perspectives on historiography become a function
of the stance adopted toward the relation between reason and revelation. In this situation, to inflate the problem of historical skepticism, making the uncertainty of all historical judgments appear to
be the main cause of the impasse between faith and history, is perhaps to avoid hard reflection on more substantive issues.

As we shall see numerous times in this study, there are other ways
in which unrefined references to Lessing's ditch can inadvertently
create more problems than they solve. The most frequent example
of this is an emphasis on the risks and corrigibility of all historical
knowledge and research in a theological situation where nothing
really depends upon historical results. In short, the successful resolution of the real theological difficulty turns out not to hang on
arriving at historical facts; to press the historiographical issue
thereby turns out to be gratuitous and misleading. We have good
reason at this point to claim that the initial source of this problem is
Lessing himself and the equivocations and abrupt transitions characterizing his "On the Proof of the Spirit and of Power." Wherever
the fault lies, however, it needs to be stressed that Lessing's ditch
comes in several forms, and that to be threatened by one of them is
not to be threatened by them all. In the absence of the clear differentiation of the several relevant issues, discussions of faith and history
in Lessing's shadow could easily turn out to be mere shadowboxing.

APPROPRIATING RELIGIOUS TRUTH:
THE "OUTER" AND THE "INNER"

To speak of the problem of religious appropriation is, first of all, to
suggest a certain distance between potential believer and religious
message. Something intrinsic to the religious message—its sheer
doubtfulness, its peculiarity or oddity, its intellectually "scandalous" character—produces this distance, thereby making religious
assent problematic and questionable, rather than automatic and
natural. Religious appropriation is the process that makes assent in
such a situation possible: it shrinks or eliminates altogether the
distance between believer and message. This does not necessarily
mean that the message is then genuinely "understood," but only
accommodated.

Obviously, the problem of religious appropriation is a continuous
theme in Lessing's "On the Proof of the Spirit and of Power." Indeed, it is perhaps the one theme holding together the discrete, and

sometimes contradictory, elements of his discussion. The temporal and metaphysical difficulties exposed by Lessing are manifestations of the appropriation issue, but they do not exhaust the possible ways of addressing the problem of distance between believer and message. For at its most comprehensive level, the appropriation issue poses a certain tension, or even an impasse, that supersedes the difficulties we have surveyed so far: it is the tension between the *implausibility* (however construed) of the religious message and the *autonomy* of the modern believer, who has the intellectual right to remain free of the heteronomous pressures exerted by appeals to unquestioned authority in religious matters. In other words, the message will prove plausible, and appropriation will become possible, only to the extent that the autonomy of the believer is protected. This means in turn that the religious message cannot be promoted, discussed, or adequately analyzed apart from anthropological inquiry into the nature of the believing self.

Understood in this way, the problem of religious appropriation is clearly not limited to questions concerning the conditions for religious assent. There is in addition a nexus of deeper, profoundly modern issues at stake here, not all of which are really grasped by Lessing. Indeed, the very notion of "appropriation" itself is potentially an anachronism when applied to Lessing. With its connotations of a latent point of contact between believer and message, the idea of appropriation perhaps makes full sense only in a post-Kantian milieu. Certainly the problem is more explicitly defined and debated in the conceptual environment produced by Hegel, Schleiermacher, and Kierkegaard.

Still, if Lessing is not an actual precursor to those confronting a bona fide "existential ditch" between message and religious self, he is on the way to becoming one because of the interplay in his thought between the motifs of "outer" and "inner." Lessing clearly wants to replace religious reliance on public, "outer" historical events and reputed miracles with reliance on the "inner" world of the moral-religious self. This "inner" world both transcends and puts into question the barriers between historical religions erected by competing confessions and doctrinal stands, the contents of which typically consist of references to the "outer" world of historical events and empirical facts. Lessing will thus appeal to the inner truth of authentic religion at the same time that he debunks public, ecclesiastical differences, a strategy typified by his play, *Nathan the Wise*.[12] Here, Moslem, Jew, and Christian find common religious ground, despite their obvious and very public "surface" differences:

"truth" in religious matters, Lessing is here saying, is a property of something intrinsic to the believers themselves—namely, sincerity and moral conduct—rather than a property of doctrinal propositions.[13] We settle the question of religious truth by looking within ourselves, not by appealing to matters of historical fact or adjudicating competing doctrinal formulations.

On this view, a depiction of religious appropriation is rendered in terms of something that is "within" the believer all along. There is for Lessing an implicit harmony between the autonomous self and the wider moral-religious universe of which the self is a part: this implicit harmony constitutes the condition of the possibility of religious appropriation.[14] Moreover, the appeal to this latent harmony between autonomous self and moral-religious universe is universalizable, despite the surface differences dividing historical religions, and thereby underwrites Lessing's commitment to religious tolerance.

Within the specific context of "On the Proof of the Spirit and of Power," this principle of universalizability is most evident in Lessing's concluding analogy, drawn from the world of mathematics.

> Suppose that a very useful mathematical truth had been reached by the discoverer through an obvious fallacy. . . . Should I deny this truth? Should I refuse to use this truth? Would I be on that account an ungrateful reviler of the discoverer, if I were unwilling to prove from his insight in other respects, indeed did not consider it capable of proof, that the fallacy through which he stumbled upon the truth *could* not be a fallacy.[15]

The intimate linkage between the truths of mathematics and the individual's capacity for grasping their apodictic certainty nicely illustrates Lessing's sense of a harmonious "fit" between self and world. Both in mathematics and in religion, "appropriation" is always potentially possible because of this hidden fit. Truth is thus not determined by the contingent, public, surface state of affairs— be it a mathematical blunder, a historical event, or a doctrinal claim; truth is instead universally present and must be carefully distinguished from our modes of access to it, which can vary enormously from one setting to the next. How we come to know the truth is, for Lessing, ultimately a matter of indifference. In his words, if a true religious teaching is conveyed by a historically dubious legend, "What does it matter to me whether the legend is false or true? The fruits are excellent."[16] What is fair for the mathematician is fair for the religious believer.

The interplay here between "outer" truth and "inner" truth illuminates the point of Lessing's metaphor of a truth that "binds."[17] Only an inner truth can be binding; that is, only a truth conveying the harmony between autonomous self and moral-religious universe binds me in a way that is free of any hint of heteronomy. The question of religious appropriation asks how I am to embrace, apprehend, or internalize a religious message that is historically dubious and, perhaps, intrinsically odd and in tension with the truths I take for granted in my everyday life. Lessing's answer comes into focus: the potential problem of plausibility haunting the religious message is put to rest by evincing the latent congruence betweeen the message and something I already and indubitably know about myself. The motif of inner truth corresponds with a rejection of heteronomy in religious matters. Applied to the specific case of Christianity and the relationship between Christian truth and traditional Christian appeals to history, Lessing's position yields his famous comment that the "letter is not the spirit, and the Bible is not religion."[18] For, as he says in editorial comments on the "Fragments" of Hermann Samuel Reimarus that Lessing brought to publication,

> the Bible obviously contains more than belongs to religion, and it is a mere hypothesis that it must be equally infallible in these extras. Moreover, religion existed before the Bible. Christianity existed before the evangelists and apostles had written. . . . The religion is not true because the evangelists and apostles taught it, but they taught it because it is true. The written traditions must be explained according to their inner truth, and no written tradition can give it any inner truth if it has none.[19]

Such a view suggests how a thinker like Lessing can retain a lively interest in Christianity and the issue of revelation, even as he rejects the historical proofs traditionally serving to underwrite Christian orthodoxy.

Lessing's appeal to the inner truth of authentic religion, and his achievement of something like a process of religious appropriation on this basis, lies somewhere between the heartfelt pietism of the Moravians, always of great interest to him, and Kant's theory of practical reason, which lay just over the horizon. In all three cases, religious belief is free from nagging empirical questions because of its self-authenticating character.[20] The religious message "makes sense"—indeed, it elicits a spontaneous and immediate recognition from the believer—because it finds purchase in the believing self.

The evasion of problems introduced by questions of historical fact and historical inquiry is secure. Once again, we discover just how artificial Lessing's original complaint about the uncertainty of all historical knowledge turns out to be. Like other Enlightenment figures, Lessing would construe the specific content of the inner truth of religion in moral terms: his "Testament of John" compresses the entire significance of Christianity into the simple formula, "Little children, love one another."[21] However, the importance of Lessing's shift from the outer to the inner transcends the moral vocabulary in terms of which he actually follows through on his insight, since nonmoral states of personal insight or consciousness could—and would—just as easily aid the final avoidance of the historical problems plaguing Christian orthodoxy. The key issue is the discovery of a surrogate for expressly historical claims in the rendering of Christian faith, a surrogate that could be defined in terms of what the believer brings *to* history, and not in terms of what history imposes on the believer.

The example of Lessing thereby suggests the intimate relationship between the appearance of new views concerning faith's relation to historical events and to historical knowledge, and the emergence of new views of the self, based on a profound confidence in human powers of self-fulfillment. Proponents of the new vision of autonomy, in terms of which Kant himself defines *Enlightenment*,[22] would naturally find unacceptably heteronomous the rigid appeal to the traditional trappings of religious positivity, such as a propositional view of revelation and the unquestioned deposit of ecclesiastical authority in scripture and tradition. For thinkers in this Enlightenment tradition, positive religion entails an objectification of religious truth that is a potential affront to the rational or moral subjectivity of the believer.

Lessing's alternative appeal to inner truth, as well as his distinction between the necessary truths of reason and the accidental truths of history, reflect his own efforts to indulge the principle of human autonomy in religious matters. An authentic religious message does not impose itself on an uncomprehending humanity, but instead finds in us an analogous structure—a natural zone of correlation or a perfectly matched receptacle—that make religious assent basically unproblematic. Closely related to this is Lessing's frequent employment of the distinction between the "letter" and the "spirit" of true religion, and his admonition always to judge the former by the latter—and his confidence that this is a straightforward task.[23] Seen in this light, the more influential Kantian theory of practical reason and Kant's application of a moral hermeneutics to scripture are, in effect, the refinement of insights already apparent in Lessing. Lessing anticipates—and, in an odd sort of way, Hegel culminates—the Kantian preoccupation with *self*-legislation in the practical arena as the chief criterion of what it means to be fully human.[24] Lukács exaggerates only slightly when he claims that religious positivity "means primarily the suspension of the moral autonomy of the subject."[25] Certainly it means the acceptance of religious truths with which I do not feel naturally comfortable. And this problem is very much at the center of Lessing's "On the Proof of the Spirit and of Power."

REDUCTIONISM AND THE
RELIGIOUS USES OF HISTORY

In his effort to find religious assurance apart from historical proofs or even from historical evidence, Lessing anticipates the basic strategy of more recent Protestant thinkers. The near unanimity with which the most influential theologians of this century have rejected the dependence of faith on historical inquiry suggests the general importance of Lessing's position. These later thinkers—such as Bultmann—obviously operate with a far more complex conceptual apparatus than does Lessing; Lessing could hardly anticipate the Kantian milieu that would define both the cognitive problems and the dualistic strategies of a later theological generation. What Lessing does share with someone like Bultmann is a loss of theological interest in those public, often miraculous historical events that constitute for a more traditionally orthodox mind the very content of Christian faith.

Thus, for Lessing as for Bultmann, virgin births, the feeding of multitudes, and dead men rising are no longer the point. References to the past—even to a seemingly miraculous past—may remain, as they do in Lessing's case; but these reported events, conveyed by scripture, are not religiously decisive for Lessing as events. Instead, these remaining references to the past become the targets of a reductionism that implicitly translates references to historical events into propositions of a nonhistorical character.[26] The references to history actually mean something else; their true meaning cannot be correctly understood apart from reference to some inherent aspect of human consciousness and to the moral-religious universe with which we are in implicit harmony, without the supposedly indispensable mediation of a particular historical event. This, finally, is the point of Lessing's distinction between outer and inner truth.

What Lessing—and thinkers after him such as Kant—are achieving through this implicit reductionism is noteworthy: they are making respectable the rejection of assent to specific statements of historical fact traditionally thought to be central to Christian faith. In light of the increasingly troublesome effects of historical biblical research in the period following Lessing and Kant, this would obviously prove to be a timely achievement. Residual historical references, particularly to Jesus, might very well remain and even hold a prominent place in the confession of faith. Such references to historical events, however, would be rendered in terms of the "deeper meaning" that is logically independent of the actual occurrence of the events referred to. Reductionism regarding historical claims would, moreover, dovetail neatly with a rejection of religious positivity, as in Lessing's own case. Consequently, historical-critical work might proceed in total freedom, but without ever becoming a theological threat. The inner truth—or deeper meaning—of faith's references to history depends on neither the occurrence of, nor inquiry into, any particular event in the past.

All of this signals the new burden automatically assumed by those, like Lessing, who turn away from the historical. This new burden concerns the responsibility to articulate the *genuine* meaning of apparent assertions of historical fact traditionally associated with the confession of faith. This in turn will require specifying the true grounds for religious assent and assurance, since sufficient evidence for decisive historical claims is no longer the pivotal issue.

As we have seen, filling the vacuum created by the rejection of historical proofs is the point of Lessing's appeal to the inner truth of religion. For Lessing and, more systematically, for Kant as well, the true locus of religious assurance is primarily moral and private, and not historical and public, in character. Yet, once again, the important thing to notice here is not so much the substitution of a moral element for the historical, but the transfer of religious interest from the public domain of external, observable events to the private, hidden domain of the believer's internal condition. Historically considered, the emergence of this new position marks the shift of modern theological concern from the objective content of faith, expressly historical in nature and concerning which the community of believers was once in unquestioned agreement, to the subjective condition of the individual believer, involving a personal, nonpublic element that can probably be neither shared nor transferred from believer to believer.

As historical events assume less and less importance for leading figures such as Lessing and Kant, experiential or intuitive states assume more importance and remain at the center of theological attention even as the specifically moral emphasis of the Enlightenment is left behind. Nonpositive, moral religion, with its reductionistic effects on history and revelation, maps out the contours of the basic theological solution to difficulties posed to Christianity by modern historical research. The structural relationship between Bultmann and Lessing is just as significant as the more frequently cited relationship between Bultmann and Kierkegaard.

The net effect of this transformation, represented by the way in which both Lessing and Kant eliminate historical difficulties, is to displace affirmations of historical fact from acounts of the chief content of faith. In their place arise implicitly self-reflexive affirmations, perhaps still clothed in historical guise. The confession of faith reveals something about the self, and perhaps something about the self's natural "fit" into a wider moral-religious world; however, the confession of faith does not provide information solely about the world, apart from all references to the confessing self.

Particularly in the philosophy of Kant, the interrelations among God, world, and self are increasingly interpreted in terms dictated by the last member of this traditional metaphysical triad, and not by the other two. A passing remark by Kant in his *Critique of Pure Reason* nicely underscores this point in a particularly telling way. Religious conviction, he tells us, "rests on subjective grounds (of the moral sentiment)," so that "I must not even say, '*it is* morally certain that there is a God, etc.' but '*I am* morally certain, etc.'"[27] The subsequent history of continental Protestant thought—running from Schleiermacher, Ritschl, and Herrmann through more recent figures such as Bultmann, Gogarten, and Tillich—represents a kind of extended commentary on this Kantian claim.[28] Some, such as Ritschl and, to a lesser extent, Herrmann, would retain and modify the moral character of faith rendered in Kantian terms. Others would replace Kant's moral emphasis with nonmoral aspects of human consciousness (often with the aid of existentialist philosophy) but without thereby ceasing to be truly Kantian, since it is the dualistic strategy and corresponding priority of the private "inner" side of this dualism, and not the strictly moral element, that defines Kantianism in these matters. The net effect of this turn inward is a commingling of God-consciousness and self-consciousness, hinted at in the above quotation from Kant and exemplified, perhaps, by the theologies of Schleiermacher and Tillich. Significantly, representatives from all sides of this post-Kantian tradition would effect their own forms of reductionism with respect to the historical referents of traditional Christian faith, taking pride in the way they salvaged faith and christology from the ravages of historical criticism. For them, faith typically gains its point by virtue of some sort of anthropological "given," in terms of which we then interpret references to history. Faith does not gain its point from the successful adjudication of matters of historical or factual detail.[29]

Lessing's reduction of historical assertions to religious affirmations of a nonhistorical sort brings into focus yet another important epistemological feature of the position on faith and history that he represents. For in rejecting the idea that Christian faith relies for its truth on inquiry into the past, thinkers in Lessing's tradition typically maintain that the true object of faith is unavailable to any form of theoretical scrutiny, historical or otherwise. In other words, it is not simply that faith is independent of the results of historical research; there is the deeper point that authentic faith repels *all* theoretical inquiry and all efforts to reformulate it in cognitive terms. In a broad sense, faith is not cognitive at all, but is more accurately characterized as "regulative" in the sense that it shapes or regulates an attitude or perspective or a mode of behavior, in contrast to faith understood as a body of beliefs that could be asserted, or rendered in paragraph form.[30] The Kantian difference between saying "It is certain" and saying "I am certain" is the difference between conveying information about the world that could, in principle, be subject to empirical checks, and saying something that cannot be understood, let alone adjudicated, apart from further information about the speaker.

In effect, then, faith in this regulative sense remains, at least to some degree, epistemologically mysterious and unaccountable. There is an important connection between the intrinsic privacy of faith—hidden from worldly scrutiny and untestable by empirical means—and the disjunction between faith and matters of historical fact. This result, in turn, is a function of the implicit tie between a theory of authentic religion and the new view of the autonomous self emerging in the eighteenth century, something that comes through more clearly (because far more systematically) in Kant's case than in Lessing's. From the newly developing perspective, disconfirmation of religious faith can never be a matter of "new information" coming in from the outside, such as the discovery that Jesus never lived. Instead, disconfirmation of faith would be more like the discovery that the self was not being true or responsible to itself, in whatever sense (for example, moral, existential) this discovery might be construed. The key issue would be "integrity" and not "facts." Kant's systematic dualisms would give particular reinforcement to this general position: the separation between theoretical and practical reason polices the dividing line between what is religiously relevant to me and what is irrelevant; and Kant's introduction of the phenomena-noumena dichotomy preserves a way of talking meaningfully about religious matters without overstepping those same cognitive boundaries to which Kant himself had taken such pains to draw our attention. Kant's notion of the noumenal protects the being and self-manifestation of God, thereby assuming the tasks traditionally ascribed to the category of the supernatural and doing so in a way that simultaneously buttresses the Protestant emphasis on the nonobjective or "subject" character of God. Likewise, the theory of the noumenal protects the interior moral and religious dimensions of the believing subject, thereby defending an autonomous human essence from theoretical intrusion and manipulation. Like Lessing's more primitive dualism between the inner and the outer, these influential Kantian dualisms thus yield a means of assuring religious certainty without accepting dependence on theoretical knowledge. Kantian strictures on the cognitive element in religious faith keep faith aloof from the give-and-take of the secular, intellectual marketplace.

In short, the turn inward toward the religious subject, reinforced in Kant's case by a dualistic epistemology, simply eliminates the religious relevance of "facts," whether they be historical or scientific. As a result, faith is not simply independent of the results of historical inquiry; from an empirical standpoint, faith is irrefutable in principle. The believer is safeguarded equally from the historian and the scientist. A basic irony of modern Christian thought resides in the eagerness with which the harshest critics of a moral or Kantian basis for theology, such as the neo-orthodox of the first half of this century, embrace and exploit this more sweeping Kantian apparatus in their conceptions of faith and revelation.

Lying in the background of these complex developments is Lessing's own reductionistic reshaping of the traditional historical content of belief, in the name of the inner truth of authentic religion. For Lessing, as for many of the post-Kantians, the lines of theological authority in the determination of true belief run from the believing subject to that which is believed, and not the other way around. The subject of faith—the one who does the believing—has the power to transform the object of faith—that which is believed—in its search for epistemological and psychological satisfaction. The converse, however, could be true only at the cost of eroding or altogether sacrificing the element of human autonomy that Lessing's notion of inner truth is designed to preserve. Consequently, on Lessing's terms, empirical inquiry into historical or scientific details never upsets the true believer. A faith that *could* be upset by such inquiry is not worth having.

Religious assurance thus becomes possible mainly because of the presence in me of what has been called an "anthropological vestibule," reflecting a Cartesian notion of the self, where the potentially strange features of the religious message are initially greeted and then clothed in terms recognizable to me.[31] Nothing can get past this vestibule that could be religiously upsetting. Primarily because of this anthropological vestibule—a metaphorical variation on what Ernest Gellner has labeled "the Protestant/Cartesian cognitive ethic"[32]—is it possible to transform a potentially dead, historical faith into a living, personal religious conviction. Through his exploitation of the motifs of "inner" and "outer," and his invocation of the metaphor of "binding," Lessing is groping for a conceptual articulation of such an anthropological vestibule, the full realization of which probably occurs only with Schleiermacher and the idealists. Lessing's ultimate reliance on a latent congruence between believing self and a wider moral-religious universe thus neutralizes potential problems posed by historical skepticism. It is this congruence that underwrites his reductionistic approach to history. Once again, we discover the artificiality of Lessing's expressions of concern over the reliability of historical reports in "On the Proof of the Spirit and of Power"—simply nothing of religious significance ultimately rides on Lessing's initial discussion of the eyewitness and noneyewitness to historical revelation. What is instead truly primary for Lessing is a principle of authenticity in religious matters that has personal immediacy—one might even say, relevance—as its chief criterion.[33] Lessing is symptomatic of modern Protestant theology generally in his readiness to transform into something else the apparently historical content of religious claims in an effort to expose their personal immediacy and, therefore, their religious authenticity. He represents the predominantly Cartesian character of this theological tradition in the way he accords to our personal mode of appropriating the religious message the dominant, controlling role in this transformation process. The position thus typified here by Lessing inevitably leads to the more recent preoccupation with hermeneutics, in which the conditions for human understanding—or appropriation—are sought in anticipation of finding the true meaning of the biblical text. The fact that the true meaning usually turns out to have little or nothing to do with the literal meaning reveals the correlation between the growing interest in hermeneutics and reductionistc approaches to the history reported in scripture.

The net result is that Lessing and others like him can afford to be cavalier about what the actual historical facts are in any given instance of biblical interpretation. After all, as the true seat of religious assurance, the interior human consciousness—however it may be specifically construed—will put the facts in their proper place, no matter what they may turn out to be. This is the advantage of a religious dwelling that includes an anthropological vestibule or anteroom.

Questions naturally arise at this point, questions which doubtless make more sense when pressed upon Lessing's successors than upon Lessing himself. The chief question concerns the point at which reductionism with respect to history puts in doubt the need for *any* historical referent for faith whatever. The tendency apparent in primitive form in Lessing—and emerging more fully in many of his Kantian successors—is to allow references to the believing self entirely to displace references to historical events in the rendering of faith. Ultimately, such a displacement process means that faith may have as its *only* content the sheer act of religious appropriation or existential self-understanding: the confession of faith becomes self-referential, virtually without remainder. In the eyes of the critic, this result empties faith of any real point. Whatever its merits, such a criticism—commonly lodged against Bultmannian theology by critics of both the left[34] and the right[35]—reveals the ironic twist attending modern Protestant efforts to neutralize the problems for faith posed by historical criticism. In avoiding the one problem— namely, the possibility that Christian faith might be subject to historiographical adjudication and even falsification—Lessing's successors have opened themselves to a new, potentially more troubling problem—that of satisfactorily answering such questions as: What states of affairs are at stake in the confession of Christian faith, other than something involving the private, religious self? What conceivable difference does it make to call oneself a "Christian?" What is the *extra me* of faith?

Such questions as these, emerging out of a consideration of how Lessing has neutralized the problem of historical-critical inquiry, are interesting not as aspects of technical, in-house, theological discussions, but as revealing indicators of the cultural significance of modern Protestant thought. In successfully putting to rest a serious and nagging intellectual difficulty, Protestant theology has introduced the prospect of its own dispensability. This is primarily due to the possibility that Protestant Christian theology does not really *assert* anything—or at least anything not being asserted quite adequately elsewhere in the culture. This possibility, in turn, bearing on the assertorial aspect of the confession of faith, is directly related to a Lessing-like eagerness to back away from factual, historical claims as the content of faith. However embarrassing or intellectually troubling those traditional references to the past were, they had the virtue of clearly identifying what it meant, cognitively at least, to be a Christian.

Thus, a consideration of Lessing's own final avoidance of historical-critical problems brings into focus the "pathos" of liberal Protestantism brought about by Protestant efforts to make peace with the general culture.[36] In the current instance, this pathos is suggested by the impasse between: having something distinctive to believe and assert, but remaining subject to empirical falsification or to charges of obscurantism and special pleading; or being comfortably continuous with the intellectual standards and demands of the wider culture, but without anything truly distinctive to assert. It is the impasse, in other words, between unintelligibility on the one hand, and dispensability on the other.[37]

Not surprisingly, it is a consideration of Kierkegaard and of his response to Lessing's ugly ditch that brings these issues into bolder relief. Kierkegaard subtly changes the nature of the debate by altering the shape of Lessing's ditch. In the process, he forces our attention in the direction of the category of "paradox," thereby putting the intelligibility issue in its modern form on the theological map. As we shall see, much recent commentary on faith and history remains largely oblivious to these Kierkegaardian alterations and to the important lessons they potentially teach.

4
Kierkegaard and the Problem of the Historical

Climacus' presentation is fatiguing, as the case required. His merit is to have "drawn" (as it is said of a telescope) the unshakable Christian fact so near to the eye that the reader is prevented from looking askant at the eighteen hundred years. His merit is by the help of dialectic to have created a view, a perspective.
— *Kierkegaard,* On Authority and Revelation

KIERKEGAARD AND LESSING'S DITCH

Through his image of the ugly ditch, Lessing has managed to convey most of the pressing difficulties attending eighteenth-century debates over the nature and possibility of revelation, the relation between faith and reason, and the connection between historical proofs and religious conviction. Moreover, Lessing's "On the Proof of the Spirit and of Power" anticipates other problems concerning theology and historical inquiry that would be of central interest during the succeeding two centuries, when the methods of modern historical research would come into their own and begin to cause serious difficulties for Christian theology. As we have seen, Lessing achieves all of this only at the cost of considerable confusion concerning, first, just which issue he is addressing at any given moment and, second, the relative degree of urgency he means to assign each of them. A clear-headed reading of his essay thus puts into question the advisability of referring to "Lessing's ditch" at all. To say this, however, is by no means to minimize the serious and lasting issues that Lessing has bequeathed to us through his image—Lessing's ditch may be highly ambiguous, but it is not unimportant.

The most famous and influential commentator on Lessing and his problems is Soren Kierkegaard. Indeed, our modern version of "Lessing's problem"—somewhat like our view of Hegel on religious matters—has been heavily filtered through a Kierkegaardian lens. In the process, Kierkegaard's work both enriches the discussion of the several issues related to the ditch and adds to the confusion. In large measure, his closely related pseudonymous works, *Philosophical Fragments* and the *Concluding Unscientific Postscript*, constitute an extended commentary on the ditch and its problems, beginning with the very title page of the *Fragments*. Yet, as we shall see, Kierkegaard does not hesitate to alter the ditch in question to suit his own purposes. Clarifying his point of departure from Lessing's *problem*, as well as his more easily grasped departure from Lessing's constructive theological position, will be the chief burden of this chapter and the next.

In the *Fragments* and the *Postscript*, Kierkegaard, like Lessing before him, addresses the relationship between faith and historical knowledge, and the problem of the subjective appropriation of religious truth. His unique treatment of these issues has of course been of lasting interest and importance. Nevertheless, it is crucial to underscore the fact that, for Kierkegaard even more than for Lessing, the dominant issue dictating his attitude toward the others is the deeper problem concerning the relation between reason and historical revelation. Kierkegaardian perspectives on positivity and christology play the controlling role in his effort to locate the wider cluster of relevant issues in a suitable configuration. Through a fresh adaptation of his frequently employed Socratic theme, Kierkegaard poses the major issues in a way that highlights the intimate connection between anthropological considerations on the one hand, and an evaluation of the meaning and point of historical revelation on the other. In stark contrast to Lessing, Kierkegaard relentlessly stresses the unique, particular, and "accidental" moment of history as decisive for faith and salvation, and then charts the eddying effects of this central commitment in his typically playful fashion.

The odd thing about Kierkegaard is the way he follows up on this firm commitment to religious positivity. For, whereas his theological dependence on a unique historical occurrence would appear to leave him reliant, at least to some degree, upon historical inquiry into the event decisive for faith—for faith must surely have an interest in whether or not the event really occurred—Kierkegaard follows Lessing in rejecting any such reliance. In this, of course, Kierkegaard anticipates and, in fact, sets the pattern for the leading Continental Protestant theologians in the years following World War I, who would accent the irreplaceable "eventful" character of historical revelation and the complete disjunction between christology and general philosophical truths, while readily joining Kierkegaard in the flight from theological reliance on historical inquiry. The resulting "Kierkegaardian model" on faith and history, in contrast to the model typified by Lessing, is a familiar one: Christian faith is decisively reliant for both its truth and its meaning upon reference to a past event; but faith is altogether independent of the ongoing results of secular, empirical inquiry into the past. Stating the matter this way helps to explain the central role played by the category of "paradox" in twentieth-century accounts of the nature of faith.

The complicating and, to some degree, ironic element here is that Kierkegaard achieves freedom from historical inquiry through much the same strategy employed by Lessing himself: he exaggerates the role played by the process of religious appropriation, through the exploitation of the existential "subject" of faith. The Kierkegaardian solution to the several problems of faith and history is thus executed by means of a radical preoccupation with the "existential ditch," where the appropriation problem resides. Taking his point of departure from his Hegelian milieu, Kierkegaard is thus able to pose the appropriation issue in a manner that is simply unavailable to Lessing. The result is the creation of a fresh orientation in religious epistemology, one that has enjoyed unparalleled influence in twentieth-century Protestant thought. A significant side effect of this Kierkegaardian triumph has been the aggressive promotion within respectable theology of fundamentally Kantian dualisms between faith and theoretical knowledge, and between God (or divine action) and observable history.

Kierkegaard's alteration of Lessing's problem is signaled at the outset by the title page of his *Philosophical Fragments*, which reads: "Is an historical point of departure possible for an eternal consciousness; how can such a point of departure have any other than a merely historical interest; is it possible to base an eternal happiness upon historical knowledge?[1] In brief compass, Kierkegaard here roves across several distinct problem areas. In contrast to Lessing's misleadingly simple formulation of his ditch, Kierkegaard's restatement of it thus indicates the complex, layered character of the difficulties at hand. This complexity is further conveyed by the way Kierkegaard treats the believer's relation to the historical within the wider context of Christianity's relationship to philosophical idealism, thereby bringing his discussion into explicit contact with the problem of reason's relation to historical revelation and the associated question of faith's relation to philosophical necessity.

Kierkegaard examines these topics as part of a broader effort to consider the question of the "truth" of Christianity. As an "objective problem," to use Kierkegaard's own expression, the truth question can be dealt with either historically or philosophically.[2] The histori-cal approach means establishing through historical methods that the events associated with the appearance of Jesus and the rise of Christianity really occurred. Put in a different idiom, the objective problem of truth in its historical aspect is a matter of adducing the appropriate external evidence for the truth claims advanced by Christianity, the issue of evidence turning on the adjudication of specific factual questions. Obviously, then, this side of the objective problem is intimately related to the concept of "proof" in religious matters, the difficulties involved in historical distance, and the reli-giously deficient character of historical reports that were all explicit topics of discussion in Lessing's "On the Proof of the Spirit and of Power."

In contrast, the philosophical aspect of the objective problem of the truth of Christianity concerns the relationship between histori-cal revelation and philosophical reason. This is not a factual or temporal problem at all, but a perennial metaphysical problem: it is the problem of correctly relating Christianity's references to the dis-crete, unique particularities of history to philosophy's traditional drive toward universal, time-invariant truths. This issue thus brings us into direct contact with those general problems of reason and revelation on the one hand, and of faith and reason on the other, that play the decisive yet often subterranean role in Lessing's essay. Likewise, the metaphysical issue puts Kierkegaard in the main-stream of nineteenth-century attempts to think through the effects of German idealism on Christian faith and theology.

Kierkegaard also speaks of the "subjective problem" of the truth of Christianity, and here, it turns out, is where his own center of interest resides. The truth of Christianity in its subjective aspect "concerns the relationship of the individual to Christianity."[3] It is not a matter of asking if Christianity is true in general or in the abstract; it is instead a matter of asking if Christianity is true "for me." Here we confront the problem of religious appropriation, con-cerning the existential ditch between myself and a dubious or strange religious message. In large part, Kierkegaard's genius lies in his suggestion that the *real* existential ditch is that between myself and a religious message that, far from being strange, has become overly familiar and repeated by rote.

As we have seen, the subjective problem—or the problem of reli-gious appropriation—lies, in primitive form, behind Lessing's doc-trine of inner truth and his effort to locate the intuitive point of contact between the believer and a "binding" religious message. In

Kierkegaard's case as well, the emphasis tips decisively in the direction of issues such as these—an obviously Lutheran ethos pervades the thinking of both of these thinkers, dictating what they take to be the truly fundamental questions for the individual believer. In effect, the general plan of Kierkegaard's *Fragments* is to pose the objective problem concerning the truth of Christianity in its starkest, most abstract form,[4] with a particular (though not exclusive) emphasis on the philosophical side of the problem, together with the beginnings of a position on the appropriation issue. As a sequel to this work, the *Postscript* completes the analysis of the historical side of the objective problem, offering Kierkegaard's most sustained account of Christianity's relation to historical knowledge, and then proceeds to a more than 400-page-long consideration of the subjective problem of appropriation, for which this book is best known. *Philosophical Fragments* is an intentionally abstract, bare-bones treatment of these problems, in which Jesus is never mentioned by name but is called the "Teacher," and in which transparent but unacknowledged references to Christianity are employed as the basis of a contrived series of dialogues which offer Kierkegaard an opportunity to deepen the irony while sharpening his genuinely serious point.[5] As one of its translators has put it, the book is constructed "in terms of imaginative hypothesis and algebraic abstraction."[6]

The *Postscript*, in turn, gives to this discussion what Kierkegaard calls its "historical costume,"[7] drawing his abstract treatment of the truth issue into explicit contact with familiar themes in the history of Christian thought. Throughout all of this, in keeping with the pseudonymous character of these works, Kierkegaard—present in the form of Johannes Climacus—retains a vaguely ironic stance toward the weighty matters at hand. His primary goal is not personal religious confession, but the clearest possible depiction of what he takes to be the Christian scheme, its relation to competing views of truth, and its relation to the existing individual.[8] For this and other reasons, Lessing's ditch here acquires the commentator it both requires and deserves—but it is also gradually transformed into an entirely fresh set of problems.

A "PROJECT OF THOUGHT"

"How far does the Truth admit of being learned?"[9] With this question, Kierkegaard sets in motion the "project of thought" constituting his *Philosophical Fragments*. The "project" character of the

work, closely related to its pseudonymous authorship, enables Kierkegaard to isolate and hold up for consideration basic features of
Christianity that, treated any other way, would appear so familiar
and commonplace as to make pointless the sustained consideration
Kierkegaard wishes to give them.

The heart of the project is a comparison of the opposing ways in
which philosophical idealism and Christianity answer the opening
question about truth. By philosophical idealism, Kierkegaard has in
mind the tradition stemming from Plato, and traceable in general
form all the way up to Hegel. By Kierkegaard's reading, this tradition holds that humankind is by nature in an immediate and essential relationship to the truth. Avenues of epistemological access
among ourselves, the world, and God are, at least in principle, always open, because of prior ontological links among all three. Accordingly, a potential "learner" of the truth needs only a Socratic
midwife as an instructor, someone who, like Socrates himself, will
"remind" me of what I already know. Such an instructor is thus
merely the "occasion" for my "recollection" of a truth from which I
am never really separated: the Socratic teacher triggers in me a
certain awareness and does not provide me with genuinely new
information.

As a result, my ignorance is always only an epistemological problem, a state of mind or consciousness, and not a state of being or
essence. Ignorance of the truth is a constantly soluble problem, and
my apprehension of the truth always takes the form of the discovery
of something I could, in principle, have known all along: "one who
is ignorant needs only a reminder to help him come to himself in the
consciousness of what he knows." The truth is not really "outside"
the learner at all, but within; the instructor exists not in an essential, decisive relation to the learning process, but only in an accidental relation to it. To grasp the truth is thus simultaneously to discover something about myself.

The alternative side of Kierkegaard's project of thought simply
translates all of these emphases into their opposites. What if I am
not in an essential and immediate relationship to the truth? What if
my ignorance results from a state of being and not simply from a
state of mind or knowing? What if learning the truth is not simply a
matter of recollecting something that I implicitly knew all along,
but involves instead the discovery of something that lies "outside"
of me?

By posing the alternatives in this uncompromising, either-or fashion, Kierkegaard at the very outset is rejecting any mediation or

common meeting point between philosophical idealism and Christianity. His project of thought admits of no middle ground. The ultimate target is not so much philosophical idealism as such, but *mediation* between philosophical reason and historical revelation—not just Hegel, but the Hegelian theological establishment of his day. If, then, I am not in an essential and immediate relation to the truth, I must be radically in "error." And, whereas to be "wrong" on the Socratic-idealist model is simply an epistemological problem—reflecting any of the several ways in which what I essentially know can be obscured, forgotten, or recondite—being wrong by the alternative model is an ontological or metaphysical problem, suggesting that I am cut off decisively from the truth in a way that is left uncorrected by even the most sustained and intensive recollection process.

In this case, apprehending the truth can hardly be a matter of self-discovery, triggered by the catalytic action of a teacher who remains of merely accidental or occasional significance. Instead, grasping the truth must involve learning something that comes from the outside. This, obviously, will require a very special sort of teacher, for this teacher must impart to me not only the truth but the "condition" necessary for understanding the truth, since otherwise my natural situation of error will invariably blind me to the truth no matter how clearly it is set before me.

> But one who gives the learner not only the Truth, but also the condition for understanding it, is more than teacher. All instruction depends upon the presence, in the last analysis, of the requisite condition; if this is lacking, no teacher can do anything. For otherwise he would find it necessary not only to transform the learner, but to recreate him before beginning to teach him. But this is something that no human being can do; if it is to be done, it must be done by the God himself.

The "condition" imparted by the incarnate God become teacher is, then, the necessary prerequisite for understanding the truth: it is what would otherwise be called "faith." Consequently, by making faith itself, as the condition or presupposition of our grasping the truth, dependent upon an external agent acting upon the believer—rather than upon the believer's discovery of a rational intuition or dimension of moral or religious insight that is already immanently lodged in the self—Kierkegaard has resolutely charted the categorical distance between the Socratic-idealist scheme and his own version of the Christian scheme. Moreover, he has posed here the general problem of reason and historical revelation in a way that correctly highlights the snug fit between this issue and anthropological considerations: whether or not the truth, and the necessary condition for appropriating it, must come from the "outside" is a function of what one understands persons to be in the first place.

Correspondingly, if the anthropological starting point dictates that the truth must come from the outside, then the teacher, far from being a mere midwife, assumes the form of a savior. A christology arising out of such a standpoint as this would therefore accentuate the themes of atonement and redemption—the inevitable result of beginning with sin rather than with ignorance. Likewise, christology in this case will affirm the traditional two natures view of the person of Jesus, since, as Kierkegaard's scheme makes clear, one who does what no human being can do must be God himself in human form. The metaphysical scandal resulting from affirming that Jesus is fully God and fully man—the eternal become the temporal—hardly threatens the coherence of this position, since the position begins with the assumption that we do not naturally have the capacity to define or even to recognize ultimate truth.

The brief dialogues between the pseudonymous author and an imaginary and increasingly impatient reader that conclude each of the chapters of *Philosophical Fragments* show clearly that Kierkegaard is not the least bit concerned about the apparent artificiality of his project of thought. His aim is to set up a contrast between two ways of appropriating the truth, and to do so in a manner that leaves no possibility of mediation between them.[10] In the process, Kierkegaard seemingly invents certain categories[11] that turn out to be thinly veiled restatements of basic Christian doctrines and concepts—a mode of operation that elicits the charge of "plagiarism" from the aroused imaginary reader.[12]

Whatever the form in which Kierkegaard has cast his project of thought, the content of the project and the stark contrasts it conveys helpfully draw *Philosophical Fragments* into intimate contact with Lessing's discussion of the ugly ditch. For the contrast between a Socratic midwife and a teacher who is "the God" is at the same time the contrast between a religion based upon reason alone and one that finds its starting point and its fundamental orientation in a historical revelation. If the learner's essential condition is one of radical error—"Let us call it Sin"—then everything must hang on the "moment" when the teacher who is God enters time, and on the "moment" when the learner receives the "condition" for grasping the truth thus revealed. Since such a historical moment is hardly a trivial matter, it "ought to have a distinctive name; let us call it the *Fullness of Time*." Furthermore, since the learner is now, in an important sense, no longer the same person, it is appropriate to call the learner "a new creature" who has experienced a "new birth." From such a standpoint, history is not "merely illustrative"— history is not "merely" anything. It is decisive.

Everything in Kierkegaard's non-Socratic scheme, then, pivots on "the historical fact that the God has been in human form." Positivity, in the orthodox form of an incarnation, and not natural modes of rationality, plays the key religious role. It is precisely the "eventful" character of this incarnation that is crucial; the accent falls on the "fact *that*." We thereby have in *Philosophical Fragments* a purely formal rendering of that exaggerated emphasis on historical revelation characteristic of Kierkegaard's position generally and particularly prominent in his attacks on the mediating theologies inspired by Hegel, in which the uniqueness and particularity of the revelatory historical moment are transmuted in terms of an overriding speculative principle.[13] For Kierkegaard, saving truth is not something we already know in principle; it is instead the product of a disruption in time which comes to us as genuinely fresh news. That such an event actually occurred is the result of a free and gracious initiative of God,[14] and not the effect of a rational and necessitated dialectic of history that can be rendered into intelligible terms by a sufficiently ambitious mode of philosophical speculation. Religious positivity thus receives Kierkegaard's full endorsement, instead of the rebuff Lessing gave it.

Because of the emphasis on divine sovereignty, historical contingency resides at the very heart of Kierkegaard's non-Socratic position. The corresponding rejection of the theological adequacy of rational thought goes hand-in-hand with the original anthropological assumption concerning our natural situation of error: if, by the terms of Kierkegaard's project of thought, we begin in error, and if, as Kierkegaard also stipulates, the responsibility for this error is somehow our own,[15] then even the most sustained speculative or moral endeavors will not qualitatively alter our situation. If we begin in error, and if we are dependent upon our own powers, then we remain in error. This situation can only be altered by a divine act that does not simply illustrate or recapitulate the primordial relation between God and humanity. And this, in turn, implies a genuinely objective ground of faith, located in a historical revelation and interpreted in terms of the implicit interplay in this scheme of the ideas of sin and grace.

The coherence of this project of thought relies heavily not only on the depiction of our situation of error, but on Kierkegaard's ascription to us of responsibility for this error. That is, the element of "willing" associated with Kierkegaard's characterization of our error bears in important ways on the nature of the solution to our dilemma, since "new information" alone—whether or not connected with an incarnation—cannot correct a willed error. Kierkegaard's reasoning at this point recapitulates that of the first chapter of Paul's letter to the Romans, where Paul depicts our own willful fall away from a natural knowledge of God. Kierkegaard likewise suggests the forfeiture of something we once had:

> In so far as the learner exists he is already created, and hence God must have endowed him with the condition for understanding the Truth. . . . But in so far as the moment is to have decisive significance (and unless we assume this we remain at the Socratic standpoint) the learner is destitute of this condition, and must therefore have been deprived of it.

To attribute this deprivation to an act of God would lead us into the contradiction that God both initially gave and then took away the condition for understanding the truth. Thus, Kierkegaard concludes—in keeping with the originating hypothesis of his project of thought—that this deprivation is our own responsibility: "Error is then not only outside the Truth, but polemic in its attitude toward it; which is expressed by saying that the learner has himself forfeited the condition, and is engaged in forfeiting it." However artificial the argumentation sustaining this claim may be, the link between our situation of error and our own act of will is crucial for Kierkegaard's project. As we shall see, attributing our error to our own act of will lies behind Kierkegaard's depiction of faith in terms of the category of paradox. His account of the origin of error thus assures that there can be no philosophical mediation to faith: viewed intellectually, faith will always be an "offense," a claim that is buttressed—and, in an odd sort of way, even explained—by the Kierkegaardian link between error and human will. Moreover, by introducing the element of will at the point of our fall into error, Kierkegaard is putting himself in position to do likewise in conjunction with his account of faith. He is, after all, on the way to depicting faith as a "leap."

In effect, then, we have here the precise opposite of Lessing's position on reason and revelation. As we have already seen, Lessing maintains that genuine religious truth has an inner rationality—and a corresponding point of contact within ourselves—and that history's proper role is purely illustrative or pedagogical. The condition of the possibility of such a scheme is a latent, harmonious congruence between believer and truth, of the sort suggested by the Socratic side of Kierkegaard's project of thought. Moreover, a historical revelation or incarnation in the traditional form in which it is construed by Kierkegaard would be interdicted by the Spinozistic metaphysical monism that evidently guides Lessing in such matters.[16] It is for such reasons as these that Lessing does not really need to worry about the historical contingency aspect of his ditch. But precisely because Kierkegaard is investing historical contingency with the maximum theological significance, he is clearly altering the stakes involved in the believer's relationship to the past.

Consequently, within Kierkegaard's scheme the modern-day believer will perhaps confront, with a genuine sense of concern and even alarm, the temporal gap between the present day and the moment when God was incarnate. Problems of historical distance and religious appropriation that were central to Lessing's discussion apparently assume here an even greater degree of urgency. Unlike Lessing—whose theory of inner truth in religious matters places him on the Socratic side of Kierkegaard's project—Kierkegaard seems at first glance to have made theology potentially dependent upon historical inquiry into the event that is decisive for faith. For whether or not God appeared in human form would seem to be a factual question, as well as a momentous one. If this is the case, then Kierkegaard apparently requires a bridge between history and religious truth in two senses, corresponding to the dual sense of history as a type of knowledge claim and as a type of event: in the first case, he seemingly needs a bridge crossing the temporal ditch, in answer to the question, "Did it really happen?"; in the second sense, he apparently needs a bridge across the metaphysical divide, in answer to the question, "How can a historical event constitute universal saving truth?" One might argue that, if these are not genuine problems requiring a Kierkegaardian solution, then history really possesses no absolute significance for the believer, in which case we are back in the situation of Socrates.

Kierkegaard certainly does not offer bridges across such ditches as these. Just here, however, in the effort to grasp what he does present instead, we confront certain confusions and, indeed, certain Kierkegaardian stereotypes. Kierkegaard himself is largely to blame for these potential misreadings, since, in a manner reminiscent of Lessing, he addresses the temporal and metaphysical ditches interchangeably: he argues the unsuitability of historical knowledge for faith at the same time that he polemicizes against Hegel's importation of necessity into the historical realm. In both cases, the dichotomy between contingency and necessity plays a crucial role. This fact, by itself, insures a measure of confusion, since the contingency-necessity distinction relates differently to epistemological issues than it does to ontological issues. Yet this confusion, in turn, is compounded by Kierkegaard's alternating treatments of history as a type of knowledge claim and as a type of event. The net effect is potentially to mislead the reader of the Climacus writings concerning Kierkegaard's reasons for separating Christian faith and historical knowledge.

It is particularly with respect to the issue of historical knowledge that Kierkegaard invites misunderstanding. He forcefully rejects any material connection between faith and historical knowledge and, with respect to the epistemology of history, he traces out a position that is virtually indistinguishable from Lessing's. Kierkegaard's language here is familiar and extremely influential, and clearly appears to be the basis of the famous Kierkegaardian impasse between the historian and the believer. Historical knowledge, he tells us, is always only an "approximation." Nothing, Kierkegaard tells us in the *Postscript*, "is more readily evident than that the greatest attainable certainty with respect to anything historical is merely an *approximation*."[17] The "most masterly historical elucidation is only the most masterly 'as good as,' an almost." Indeed, "if all the angels in heaven were to put their heads together, they could still bring to pass only an approximation, because an approximation is the only certainty attainable for historical knowledge." Not surprisingly, then, historical knowledge is hardly the sort of thing with which faith could enter into a comfortable partnership since faith, claims Kierkegaard, "is by no means partial to probability: to make such an assertion about Faith is to slander it."[18]

We seem to have here a reasonably straightforward point, one which is particularly familiar because of numerous twentieth-century variations on it. Historical research provides only probabilities, in the form of corrigible empirical claims that are always open to future change and correction. Faith can hardly be expected to rest comfortably on such a basis. Thus, faith and historical knowledge are, in principle, incommensurate.

What needs to be stressed, however, is that the incommensurability between faith and historical knowledge is for Kierkegaard *not* due to the "merely approximate" character of historical knowledge. Faith is indeed insulated from historical inquiry for Kierkegaard, but not for reasons of historical epistemology. As we shall see, the decisive aspect of the historical event crucial for faith and salvation—namely, God's appearance as a man—is not the sort of thing worldly eyes could ever detect: it is a historical event that has no possible historiographical accompaniment. Consequently, whether or not historical knowledge is merely approximate and contingent turns out to be beside the point.

Correctly grasping the true grounds for the Kierkegaardian impasse between faith and historical knowledge thus depends upon seeing how he reshapes the ugly ditch in question, leaving behind the distinction between contingency and necessity in the process. For even though, like Lessing, Kierkegaard is employing this distinction when he characterizes historical knowledge as merely approximate (that is, contingent), he is *not* invoking this distinction when he states what he identifies as the basic problem of the ditch. Instead he poses the problem in terms of the dichotomy between historical contingency (or temporality) and *eternity*, which comes to expression most forcefully in his understanding of the incarnation and which dominates the famous title page of *Philosophical Fragments*.

Thus, the decisive ditch for Kierkegaard is not the temporal-factual one, for in that case the eyewitness to the incarnation would have a religious advantage, a possibility, as we shall see, that Kierkegaard specifically repudiates. Nor is the key issue the ditch between historical contingency and philosophical necessity, for then Kierkegaard would be committed to saying that authentic religious truth is necessary in character—just the result he wants to avoid, given his anti-Hegelian emphasis on the free initiative of a sovereign God and his non-Socratic emphasis on the historical moment.

Instead, the decisive ditch for Kierkegaard, arising out of the temporality-eternity dichotomy, involves the incommensurability between historical judgments and dogmatic christological claims, an impasse that is implicitly fundamental to Lessing's discussion but only episodically and confusingly explored by him. As we shall see, Kierkegaard resolves this problem—in a manner that leaves the believer independent of historical inquiry—by exploiting the theme of religious appropriation. Grasping his subtle transformation of Lessing's problem, and appreciating the full contours of a position on faith and history that would have far more impact than Lessing's, therefore requires a closer examination of Kierkegaard's understanding of history, his view of the relation between history and philosophical necessity, and his understanding of where genuine incommensurability in these matters really lies.

THE NATURE OF THE HISTORICAL

We have seen that Lessing employs the distinction between contingency and necessity in at least two ways: explicitly, when he is characterizing the contingent, accidental nature of historical truths, with the resulting incommensurability between history and the necessary truths of reason; and implictly, when he smuggles in his commitment to the necessary character of authentic religious truth. Insofar as this position effectively gives Lessing a secure foothold on the necessity side, it becomes apparent that there is something artificial and perhaps even forced and purely tactical about his expressions of anxiety about crossing the ditch.

Kierkegaard also employs the contingency-necessity distinction in his discussion of historical knowledge. However, the implications of his analysis of historical knowledge in terms of its accidental, contingent, or "merely approximate" character clearly set his position away from Lessing's, since, in contrast to the Socratic-idealist scheme, Kierkegaard embraces a particular historical moment—the incarnation—as theologically determinative. Consequently, one might justifiably expect that his analysis of historical knowledge would ultimately be aimed at showing its suitability as a partner for faith, a faith that is, after all, animated by a unique historical event and not by a universal and necessary truth of reason. But precisely the opposite occurs. Even though Kierkegaard, unlike Lessing and his idealist successors, does not seek theological refuge in necessity, he offers us an even deeper incommensurability between faith and historical knowledge than does Lessing himself. The important and often misunderstood feature of this result is that it does not arise from considerations of historical epistemology. In other words, nothing of a truly *theological* importance finally rides on Kierkegaard's famous and highly influential characterization of historical knowledge as "mere approximation knowledge."

A consideration of what Kierkegaard means by history, or the historical, will begin to make this clear. Precisely at that point in *Philosophical Fragments* when the decisive importance of history for the non-Socratic position has become unmistakable, Kierkegaard offers us an "Interlude" in which the nature of the historical is closely scrutinized.[19] It is an important, if turgid, piece of writing.

Unlike Lessing, who continually equivocates between history as a type of event and history as a type of knowledge, Kierkegaard at least distinguishes between these two differing senses of the historical even as he alternates his references to them. In the process, he makes our understanding of the epistemological aspect dependent upon a prior rendering of the actualities constituting the events referred to by the knowledge claims; his theory of historical knowledge presupposes his theory about what historical "events" are. Kierkegaard stipulates that historical events or actualities always involve "a coming into existence," a form of transformation distinct from the lock-step transitions characteristic of formal logic and therefore lacking the epistemological certainty enjoyed by logic. Kierkegaard wants to say that the world of logic leaves everything as it is; authentic "change" occurs only in the historical realm.

Expressed differently, Kierkegaard's point is that the necessities of logic and the contingencies of history never find a meeting point. The difference between the two, Kierkegaard says in quoting Aristotle, involves a "metabasis eis allo genos"—the very same Aristotelian quotation employed by Lessing in his discussion of the ugly ditch. Kierkegaard maintains that the "non-being" out of which a change involving a coming into existence arises is something that we can give a name to: it "is precisely what possibility is." Because something that enjoys actual existence is what we mean by actuality, "the change of coming into existence is a transition from possibility to actuality."

Kierkegaard's introduction here of the category of possibility is decisive. It is what enforces the stringent dualism characterizing his analysis, since, after all, we could not say that necessity possesses possibility without robbing both terms of their most basic meanings. However, since for Kierkegaard every change that involves a coming into existence begins in possibility, we must conclude that necessity can never come into existence. The ejection of necessity from the historical realm, set up by Kierkegaard's employment of the category of possibility, has been triggered. Necessity is, on these terms, utterly incommensurate with the event form of the historical, a conclusion that simply echoes in greater detail Lessing's position: "Everything which comes into existence proves precisely by coming into existence that it is not necessary, for the only thing which cannot come into existence is the necessary, because the necessary *is*." And, if no coming into existence ever involves necessity, then *every* coming into existence must involve freedom. A particular coming into existence may *seem* to be necessitated, but only because of a certain illusion occasioned by the intervening causality which can make a specific event appear to be the necessary result of a chain of cause and effect. Yet, claims Kierkegaard, the intervening causes have themselves come into existence in a way that untimately points back to a freely effecting cause.

Kierkegaard is offering us here a cumbersome mixture of anti-Hegelian parody and serious philosophical intent. He is also exploiting the historical issue in a way that allows him to work through in yet another format the topic of freedom and necessity, a subject very central to his entire *oeuvre*. And, at a deeper, theological level, he is implicitly reflecting on what it might mean to take with utmost seriousness the doctrine of God as creator—the one truly ultimate freely effecting causal agent.

Despite these several levels of meaning, however, the epistemological implications of Kierkegaard's view of history are reasonably clear. If history is constituted by the free and contingent transition from possibility to actuality—if, in other words, a coming into existence is the "decisive historical predicate"—then history obviously offers us no absolute certainties, if the relevant paradigm of certainty is logical necessity. Precisely because historical events or actualities involve a coming into existence that is incommensurate with necessity, historical *knowledge* must always retain an element of doubt and uncertainty. The possibilities inherent in history as a type of event introduce a permanent corrigibility into history considered as a type of knowledge. Lessing was right: a contingent truth of history can never serve as the proof of a necessary truth of reason. The possibility of error invariably lingers in every claim we might make about the past, no matter how strong the consensus concerning any particular claim may be. To be altogether free from any chance of error would require that we exist in the world of logic, not history.

At first glance such a result as this would appear to offer an epistemological advantage to an actual eyewitness to a historical event, and a corresponding advantage to an eyewitness to the revelatory events that are crucial in the non-Socratic scheme of Kierkegaard's project of thought. Someone who could believe his or her eyes and ears would not be subject to the vicissitudes of historical reconstruction; an eyewitness to the life and deeds of Jesus would not be dependent upon the testimony of scripture. If this is the case, then the only ditch confronting Kierkegaard would be the purely temporal-factual one, concerning which immediate, firsthand experience becomes the epistemological ideal for the religious believer.

We shall momentarily have occasion to consider in detail Kierkegaard's position on the theme of "contemporaneity." For now, however, it is simply important to stress that, in his discussion of history as distinct from logic, Kierkegaard is effectively proposing a general theory of empirical knowledge and not simply a theory of our knowledge of the past. The epistemological contrast in the "Interlude" of *Philosophical Fragments* is not between immediate experiential knowledge and the reconstruction of the past into historical claims, as though those persons closer to the events in question are closer to epistemic certainty. Instead, the contrast is between logically necessary knowledge and knowledge that is only contingently true. Indeed, Kierkegaard maintains that, although we can directly experience the immediate presence of something that has come into existence, we *cannot* experience the actual coming into existence itself which constitutes the very essence of the historical. In an interesting way, Kierkegaard's position here corresponds to Hume's analysis of causality, with its suggestion that we never really experience a "cause" but only a regular succession of events into which we then read the category of causality.[20] All knowledge of coming into existence, then, is in effect inferential in nature, derived from our more immediate knowledge of what is. According to the terms of Kierkegaard's "Interlude," however, knowledge of what simply is cannot be equated with knowledge of a coming into existence, which is the decisive mark of the historical. The potential epistemological hazards with which this confronts the knower are thus shared by eyewitness and noneyewitness alike. The eyewitness may enjoy a somewhat safer (because shorter) inferential route, but the possibility of error in claims to historical knowledge nonetheless remains.

It is because historical knowledge never arises out of directly experiencing what Kierkegaard calls a coming into existence that he introduces the category of "belief."[21] Indeed, the ponderous argumentation of the "Interlude" may simply be a strategy for attending to this category and to the difference between belief in normal instances of historical knowledge and belief in connection with the event of the incarnation.[22] Belief, Kierkegaard tells us, is "the organ for the historical" that has as its chief task the negation of the residue of uncertainty always accompanying efforts to apprehend a coming into existence.[23] In other words, belief is a kind of suppressant: it is the capacity to annul doubt. This can occur, not through an intellectual act of the understanding, but only through an exercise of the will—"belief is not a form of knowledge, but a free act, an expression of will," says Kierkegaard. "It believes the fact of coming into existence, and has thus succeeded in overcoming within itself the uncertainty that corresponds to the nothingness of the antecedent non-being. . . ." Belief counteracts the fact that we can never immediately and noninferentially know a coming into existence. Accordingly, the "conclusion of belief is not so much a conclusion as a *resolution*, and it is for this reason that belief excludes doubt."

The introduction of an act of will or resolution here has important consequences. Hermann Diem argues that Kierkegaard's rendering of historical knowing in these terms simultaneously puts before us two questions that are normally treated separately: first, "the question of the historical actuality of events"; second, "the question of my personal relation to them."[24] By introducing an act of will as mediator between myself and the past, Kierkegaard has not simply shown what is for him the basis of historical knowledge; rather, he has done so in a way that forces us to take a stand, or adopt a position, with respect to any potential instance of historical knowing. Genuine *historical* knowing, according to the terms Kierkegaard has laid out in the "Interlude," would by definition involve apprehending a coming into existence, which for Kierkegaard is the decisive predicate of the historical. However, we possess no faculty for grasping a coming into existence. By Kierkegaard's own account, we can experience only the results or effects of the genuinely historical, and this through the immediate cognition of what simply "is." From this empirical immediacy, we then infer *back* to the antecedent coming into existence, with the help of "belief," and thereby acquire historical knowledge.

Such a theory of historical knowledge thus means that the knower is always once-removed from the truly historical. The point of the category of belief is to mediate between the knower and the historical. We can no more have direct, unmediated knowledge of the historical, understood in Kierkegaard's terms, than the Humean knower can have a direct and unmediated knowledge of causality. Belief in Kierkegaard's sense involves intentionality, however, which is why historical knowledge on these terms prohibits neutrality and draws together the questions of the actuality of a past event and my personal attitude or response to it. Pushed to the extreme, this could mean that if I am truly to grasp the historical, I must first transpose a putative past event "back into the reality of its [original] becoming, in order to appropriate it and fulfill it as a possibility in [my] own life of decisive becoming" and willing.[25] In other words, authentic historical knowing might require something like the reenactment of the event known.[26] This becomes especially and more momentously true if we adopt an expressly ethical standpoint toward the past, for from an ethical point of view "any mere examination of the historical is excluded, because the historical always implies a reality that has been purchased by thought and is vitally related to my own personal reality in that it summons me to realize its possibilities."[27]

Obviously, this point is intensified within the expressly *religious* dimension of existence that Kierkegaard is exploring in conceptual form in his Johannes Climacus works. Here the whole point is to prod or sting the reader into a new relationship with the familiar data of Christianity, data that had been robbed of significance through sheer over-familiarity. In these religious matters, as elsewhere, true apprehension of the historical insinuates a coming into existence into one's own life, which is to say, a personal transformation—a "new birth."[28] Kierkegaard's theory of historical knowledge thereby meshes neatly with his rendering of faith in terms of becoming contemporaneous with Christ.[29] Existentialist historiography neutralizes the effects of the passage of time, or of what Kierkegaard refers to as the "1800 years."[30]

Kierkegaard's explication of the historical both as a matter of determining "what happened" *and* as a kind of summons to realize new possibilities in one's own life is the basis of familiar conceptions of historicity underwriting much twentieth-century theology. However, the point that Diem draws from Kierkegaard's account is a telling one: he suggests that, within this Kierkegaardian historiography, "the question of the *actuality* of an event is of minor importance, for it contributes nothing to the understanding of the historical" in the sense most important to Kierkegaard.[31] In other words, Kierkegaard's theory of the existentialist pay-off of a historical event, based on rendering the original occurrence of becoming in a fresh way in one's own existence—since otherwise one is cut off from the truly historical and is left only with its "effects," or with sheer "immediacy"—threatens to make irrelevant the question of whether or not the original event actually occurred. What becomes important is what I do in my own life of willing and decision making, and not "what happened" apart from me in the past.

Kierkegaard's general position on empirical knowledge appears, then, to put an eyewitness and a noneyewitness on a more equal epistemological footing than the temporal distance between them would initially suggest. The inability really to "know" a coming into existence affects eyewitness and noneyewitness alike. What common sense might construe to be firsthand experience of something that can only be remembered by others through historical reconstruction is called by Kierkegaard "the immediacy of sense and cognition, in which the historical [as such] is not contained."[32] On this view, the immediacy of sense and cognition that characterizes the situation of the eyewitness is in no way superior to "the immediacy of testimony" which serves a later generation as their mode of access to the past.

> A successor believes, to be sure, on account of the testimony of some contemporary; but only in the same sense as a contemporary believes on account of his immediate sensation and immediate cognition. But no contemporary can believe by virtue of this immediacy alone, and neither can any successor believe solely by virtue of the testimony to which he has access.[33]

Such a position means, of course, that it makes no sense to argue that faith cannot rest on historical knowledge on the grounds that historical results are always unnecessary, approximate, and relative, as though the relevant contrast case were some kind of certainty enjoyed by an eyewitness. Such an argument would, to borrow Arthur Danto's example, be like saying it is sad to be a Frenchman because all Frenchmen die.[34] The reasons that the noncontemporary has to be worried about the certainty of historical knowledge apply to the contemporary as well. The theological irrelevance of historical knowledge must therefore have its source somewhere other than in a certain flaw attending historical reconstruction, a flaw that would give a decisive advantage to an eyewitness. For if the eyewitness does *not* have an epistemological advantage, then the corrigibility and uncertainty of historical knowledge cannot be the reason for its incommensurability with faith. And, unless Kierkegaard's comments about history yielding mere approximation knowledge are purely gratuitous, then the point of such comments must not really be to fashion a position on faith's relation to historical knowledge. Instead, Kierkegaard's position regarding this relation must reflect a deeper commitment on his part, regarding which his comments about historical research are merely illustrative and not constitutive.

5
History and Paradox

So much depends, when we wish to unite two good things, upon the order in which they are united.
    —*Kant*, Religion Within the Limits of Reason Alone

FAITH AND THE HISTORICAL

The real clue for grasping Kierkegaard's reasons for separating faith and historical knowledge, despite the fact that faith demands reference to a historical event, lies in his view of faith. This becomes particularly evident in his discussion of the theme of "contemporaneity" in *Philosophical Fragments*, where Kierkegaard makes it clear that, whatever advantages an eyewitness to the incarnation might have, they are not religious advantages. It is just here, in his discussion of the contemporary disciple and what he calls the disciple "at second hand," that Kierkegaard orchestrates the complex set of categories that insures the divorce between faith and historical research, even though faith remains reliant for both its truth and its meaning upon a historical occurrence. The effect of these categories is readily apparent in his claim that "the knowledge of some historical circumstance, or indeed a knowledge of all the circumstances with the reliability of an eye-witness, does not make such an eyewitness a disciple; which is apparent from the fact that this knowledge has merely historical significance for him."[1] Indeed, Kierkegaard goes on, we observe that "the historical in the more concrete sense is *a matter of indifference*." The nonbeliever may in fact possess a far greater store of historical detail, or even of immediate, firsthand experience, than the genuine believer. The eyewitness may in turn be a true disciple, but not by virtue of being an eyewitness. For faith, says Kierkegaard, "cannot be distilled from even the nicest accuracy of detail."

It is crucial to notice here that Kierkegaard is not simply stating in another way the claim that historical knowledge is mere approximation knowledge. He is not, in other words, squeezing a theological result from an analysis of historical existence and its characteristic epistemological features. He is instead making the far more radical claim that historical knowledge *as such* is "a matter of indifference." This immediately shifts the issue to quite a different level, for any niceties of epistemological detail connected with a discussion of historical knowledge are completely neutralized—because superseded—by the claim Kierkegaard is putting before us here. We are not dealing with degrees of certainty, but with absolute impasse.

Historical knowledge does not become a matter of indifference for the believer because it is merely approximate and always subject to change and correction. That it is a matter of indifference stems from Kierkegaard's understanding of faith, which resists any point of contact with historical knowledge whether or not it is mere approximation knowledge. This is because Kierkegaard takes pains in *Philosophical Fragments* to render faith in terms of his category of paradox, and once he introduces this notion, it will hardly matter what sort of knowledge historical research yields, since the basis for an irremediable impasse between faith and any sort of knowledge is thus assured.

Kierkegaard renders faith paradoxically, thereby setting it in a polar relationship with any form of knowledge whatever, because of the terms dictated by his project of thought. This brings us to the main point: the constitutive issue in Kierkegaard's divorce between faith and historical knowledge is not the always doubtful character of historical results; rather, it is his originating, non-Socratic hypothesis concerning our situation of error. Kierkegaard is seeking out a means of resolving the basic dilemma with which the non-Socratic scheme confronts us—namely, the dilemma of showing how we might come to know what, by our very nature, we cannot possibly know.

In other words, Kierkegaard is simply thinking through to its appropriate and radical conclusion the requirement that both the truth, and the condition for appropriating the truth, come from outside of the believer. The difficulty concerns establishing some sort of avenue between believer and saving truth, in the context of our condition of error or sin. The language of paradox naturally arises as the appropriate technical idiom within which to explore this situation in which the believer originally possesses neither the truth nor an intuitive, rational capacity for recognizing or appropriating the truth: paradox talk fills the vacuum created when the Socratic-idealist scheme is displaced by Kierkegaard's uncompromising alternative.

This discussion is not the place to become bogged down in an exhaustive account of Kierkegaard's controversial employment of the idea of paradox. In its most general sense in *Philosophical Fragments*, however, this category always signals "something that thought cannot think." If thought *could* think whatever it is that the paradox is or conveys, then we would be back in the Socratic-idealist scheme, with its network of internal connections and corridors running between self, world, and God. We would enjoy the advantages of Lessing's "anthropological vestibule," where any conceivable datum is received and, if necessary, translated into recognizable form according to the dictates of a natural rationality. It is in terms of such a procedure that a natural theology or philosophy of religion transforms or eliminates altogether the scandal of the Christian message. Special revelation is rendered in terms of general revelation; nature is emphasized over grace.

Kierkegaard, of course, will have none of this. The whole point of his project of thought is to repudiate precisely those efforts to mediate Christianity and philosophical idealism that constitute a classic example of an anthropological vestibule at work. Mediating efforts are covert forms of "domestication," the aim of which is to make Christianity "easier," and, as Kierkegaard likes to remind us, he has determined that his own life's work lies in making things "harder."[2] Consequently, whatever the notoriously varying nuances of his employment of the idea of paradox may be,[3] his use of it always involves the confrontation between natural modes of human apprehension and something with which they are totally incommensurate. In this sense, as Kierkegaard himself points out, the idea of paradox is not really a "concession," denoting a failure of intellectual nerve and legitimating the charge of irrationalism; it is instead a "category," which has an altogether fitting and appropriate application for any thinker committed to thinking through the limits of the human intellect.[4] Its role is analogous to that played by the notion of "dialectic" in Kant's philosophy: it is a device for marking out an intellectual boundary line. Mapping or charting these intellectual limits, and finding a way of talking about them that does not rob them of their point by assuming knowledge of what lies on both sides of the limits, will obviously have a central place in the non-Socratic part of the project of thought. Worded somewhat differently, the category of paradox is the Kierkegaardian substitute for the Hegelian principle of identity: it reinforces, rather than resolves, the relevant dialectical tensions.[5]

In *Philosophical Fragments* Kierkegaard explores the idea of paradox along two fronts, one ontological and the other epistemological. Both aspects contribute to the eventual incommensurability between faith and historical knowledge. In the ontological sense, where the problem of history in its event or actuality aspect resides, Kierkegaard poses the "absolute paradox" that God entered time.[6] The chief dualism running through Kierkegaard's thinking comes into full play here. As a fusing of temporality and eternity in one genuinely historical moment, the incarnation requires its own unique category so that its impossible character might be highlighted. This, thinks Kierkegaard, must be stressed in opposition to the Hegelian demonstration of the rational unification of the transcendent and the immanent, a demonstration that subordinates the divine mystery and initiative to a metaphysical scheme. The fusing of temporality and eternity is what Kierkegaard means to convey by his notion of the "moment" taken in one of its senses: the appearance of God in time. The moment, says Kierkegaard, is the paradox "in its most abbreviated form." The epistemological fallout of this is reason's inevitable collision with "offense," the unhappy encounter with paradox that makes reason itself "absurd" and "a blockhead and a dunce" due to its inability to penetrate the incarnation. Both the event of God's entering time, and the appropriation of this occurrence by the believer, must be rendered in a way that does justice to their nonrational character: the requirements of the non-Socratic standpoint have pushed us toward something that reason could not predict and which it cannot now digest. If at any point Kierkegaard modifies in the slightest way his emphasis on the absolute otherness of God and the complete absence in us of a natural capacity for grasping the incarnation, then we fall back into the Socratic-idealist scheme.

The point, then, is that both the content of faith and the fact that there is such a thing as faith at all must be posed in a manner consistent with these non-Socratic requirements, and this is the task assigned to the category of paradox.[7] The content of faith is the fact that God has entered time, something that repels any effort to translate it into terms provided by speculative thought: "The historical fact that the God has been in human form is the essence of the matter."[8] Faith, as the only possible epistemological counterpart of this event, cannot be "a form of knowledge." nor even "an act of will." Indeed, faith cannot be continuous with any inherent structure of human reason, experience, or moral consciousness—it occupies no space in an anthropological vestibule.

Instead, faith is a "third entity," in addition to reason and paradox, which effects the union of learner and paradox once reason has been found wanting for this task and has been "set aside." Accordingly, since "no knowledge can have for its object the absurdity that the Eternal is the historical," and since precisely this absurdity is the content of a faith that satisfies the demands of the non-Socratic scheme, then faith itself is as much a paradox as the incarnation. Kierkegaard underscores this conclusion in his observation that "all that holds true of the Paradox holds true of Faith."[9] Our relationship to saving truth cannot be rendered naturally, mediated philosophically, or proven historically. It can only be described paradoxically and—as the *Postscript* to *Philosophical Fragments* makes abundantly clear—appropriated subjectively.

In his notion of faith we meet Kierkegaard's category of the "moment" in its second sense. It is the point in time when the believer truly grasps or apprehends that God has entered time (the event constituting the moment in its initial sense), an apprehension that produces a "new creature" through a "new birth." The moment of faith—and not rational insight, philosophical wisdom, or historical knowledge—defines the true disciple.

> How does the learner then become a disciple? When the Reason is set aside and he receives the condition. When does he receive the condition? In the Moment. What does the condition condition? The understanding of the Eternal. But such a condition must be an eternal condition.—He receives accordingly the eternal condition in the Moment, and is aware that he has so received it; for otherwise he merely comes to himself in the consciousness that he had it from eternity. It is in the Moment that he receives it, and from the Teacher himself.[10]

This meshing of the one sense of the moment—the point in time when God becomes temporal—with the other—the point in time when the believer receives the condition of faith—is the centerpiece of Kierkegaard's non-Socratic, anti-idealist position in *Philosophical Fragments*. By neutralizing the effects of the intervening "1800 years," and by resisting the cultural "naturalization" or domestication of the Christian "fact," the category of the moment sustains Kierkegaard's understanding of Christian existence in terms of becoming contemporaneous with Christ. It should be clear that, despite its connotations, Kierkegaard's moment is not really a quantitative category at all, denoting a certain duration of time. It is instead a primarily qualitative term, denoting a radical disruption, alteration, or transformation, one that submits to no speculative smoothing out, or philosophical translation. Kierkegaard's moment is meant to convey the ontological contradiction of the incarnation, and the life-altering shock of faith, without rationalizing either. It is a key theme in Kierkegaard's attack on what he takes to be idealism's falsification of the nature of existence itself, as well as in his efforts to demarcate the specific character of Christian existence.

In the "Interlude" of *Philosophical Fragments*, Kierkegaard finds further reason to underscore the completely unique character of faith. This concerns the special relation in which faith stands to the historical. We have seen that, for Kierkegaard, genuine apprehension of the historical always requires an act of "belief," since the coming into existence that defines the historical is never accessible to immediate sensation or cognition. Belief, as an act of the will, is required to offset the element of doubt remaining in any attempt to apprehend the genuinely historical.

As a historical event, the incarnation will presumably be an instance of this scheme and will demand of us the requisite act of belief. However, as Kierkegaard's category of absolute paradox makes clear, we are dealing here with no ordinary historical event; consequently, ordinary belief will, in this case, be insufficient. Such a result is readily apparent in light of the fact that belief in the ordinary sense is defined in terms of the act of will necessary to annul doubt, while faith, by contrast, is not "an act of will."

An event such as the absolute paradox of the incarnation will require instead what Kierkegaard calls belief "in the eminent sense," by which he means the sense in which the word may be used in connection with only one relationship—that of the believer to the fact of God's having entered time. Kierkegaard employs the same term (*Tro*) when discussing belief "taken first in the direct and ordinary sense, as the relationship of the mind to the historical," and belief taken "in the eminent sense," in connection with the very special coming into existence constituted by the incarnation.[11] However, to draw out the difference between the two and to underscore the sense of the latter usage, Swenson has translated belief "in the eminent sense" as "faith": belief as "faith" denotes the singular apprehension of a historical event that has as its content the contradiction that the eternal has become temporal.[12] The nature of the event in question resists all natural modes of speculation and reflection, including the act of will characterizing belief in the direct and ordinary sense. The incarnation demands its own unique epistemological category, unaccounted for by human intentions or capacities, since otherwise we risk slipping back again into the Socratic-idealist mode.

CONTEMPORANEITY

Kierkegaard's stance prompts him to fashion a fresh conception of contemporaneity itself, something for which he remains extremely influential. A true contemporary, Kierkegaard finally argues in *Philosophical Fragments,* is not the eyewitness at all; rather, it is one who receives the condition of faith from God and, through faith, believes that God has assumed human form, that the eternal has in fact become temporal.[13] The difference between contemporary and noncontemporary to *this* event is not a chronological difference—the main problem posed by Lessing's ditch is never understood by Kierkegaard to be a chronological or temporal one. Instead, to be truly contemporaneous with the incarnation is to possess the "eyes of faith,"[14] and faith, says Kierkegaard, is a "passion" which is misdirected when it takes "the merely historical as its object." "If our fact is assumed to be a simple historical fact, contemporaneity is a desideratum." We have seen, however, that the object of faith is no simple historical fact at all, but is "the absolute fact" which involves a self-contradiction. Such a content as this exists only for faith, which is contingent upon receiving the condition from God, and not upon one's chronological relation to the event in question. The paradoxical character of faith's object "cancels the difference which exists for those of diverse temporal situations."

The upshot is that, for Kierkegaard, there really is no "disciple at second hand" at all.

> The first and the last are essentially on the same plane, only that a later generation finds its occasion in the testimony of a contemporary generation, while the contemporary generation finds this occasion in its own immediate contemporaneity. . . . But this immediate contemporaneity is merely an occasion, which can scarcely be expressed more emphatically than in the proposition that the disciple, if he understood himself, must wish that the immediate contemporaneity should cease, by the God's leaving the earth.

Significantly, the only role played by contemporaneity in the familiar, chronological sense is that of analogue to the contemporary's own testimony to a later generation: contemporaneity itself, like the contemporary's testimony to a later, noncontemporary generation, is merely the "occasion" for faith, and not the basis or cause of faith.[15] The only thing the contemporary can do for the successor is "inform him that he has himself believed this fact, which is not in the strict sense a communication . . . but merely affords an occasion."[16] This is precisely the role played by firsthand experience as well: "One who is not contemporary with the historical has, instead of the immediacy of sense and cognition, in which the historical is not contained, the testimony of contemporaries, to which he stands related in the same manner as the contemporaries stand related to the said immediacy." Since we are dealing here with no simple historical fact, but with a historical fact which can become an object only for faith and "which one human being cannot communicate to another," contemporary and noncontemporary alike are dependent upon receiving the eyes of faith, through which alone the true believer "sees." Says Kierkegaard, "Only one who receives the condition from God is a believer."

Kierkegaard thus draws on the unique character of faith's object as a way of neutralizing the effects of temporal distance. He is simultaneously demonstrating the indispensability of a historical moment for faith *and* the irrelevance of empirical inquiry into that historical moment. Invariably, such a position forces Kierkegaard into a delicate balancing act, one that is reflected in his comment that the "historical aspect must indeed be accentuated, but not in such a way that it becomes decisive for the individual . . . [but] neither may the historical aspect be eliminated, for then we have only an eternal fact," which, as Kierkegaard himself points out, would leave us back with Socrates. In other words, the elimination of the difference between eyewitness and noneyewitness—executed so that the believer has total independence from the historian— must not procede in a way that entails the elimination of a historical reference point for faith. The danger, as Kierkegaard correctly sees, is that the strategy designed to gain theological freedom from historical research potentially jeopardizes the strategy designed to refute the Socratic-idealist position. After all, one consequence of the Socratic-idealist scheme is to make all persons equidistant from the truth, and thus independent of all historiographical labors— which is exactly what Kierkegaard wants to achieve in his revision of the notion of contemporaneity.

Kierkegaard concludes his consideration of contemporaneity with a clarification of just what sort of reference to the past faith actually needs. His comment is a precursor of twentieth-century appeals to the kerygma about the risen Christ, rather than to the words and deeds of the historical Jesus himself.

> If the contemporary generation had left nothing behind them but these words: "We have believed that in such and such a year the God ap-

peared among us in the humble figure of a servant, that he lived and taught in our community, and finally died," it would be more than enough. The contemporary generation would have done all that was necessary; for this little advertisement, this *nota bene* on a page of universal history, would be sufficient to afford an occasion for a successor, and the most voluminous account can in all eternity do nothing more.

Kierkegaard is again underscoring his claim that, like literal contemporaneity itself, the testimony to a noncontemporary generation is simply the "occasion" for faith and not its cause. The reference to the past takes on the role of Socrates, but in the name of a non-Socratic cause.

The net effect of Kierkegaard's reflections on the theme of contemporaneity is to underscore his main point—namely, that faith is a paradox. There is no natural mediation to faith, whether through the universal verities of philosophical wisdom or through historical reconstruction. In the context of Kierkegaard's several methods for stressing this point, and in light of the intimate relationship between the category of paradox and the requirements of a ruthlessly consistent non-Socratic scheme, the true source of the incommensurability between faith and historical knowledge gradually comes into focus. It has nothing whatever to do with the "merely approximate" or corrigible character of historical knowledge; that epistemological issue is a dead letter by this point. The impasse between faith and historical knowledge is instead a function of both the non-Socratic hypothesis concerning our situation of error and the utter dichotomy between temporality and eternity in terms of which Kierkegaard thinks through the resulting relationship between ourselves and the truth.

This Kierkegaardian impasse thus turns out to be simply one member of a large class of epistemological results produced by his project of thought. Kierkegaard has not set out to establish "a position" on faith and history at all. That he has a position on this topic is mainly the accidental by-product of his effort to emphasize the odd character of faith. It is odd because of the categories Kierkegaard must devise when attempting to set up a consistent alternative to the Socratic-idealist model, categories that accommodate the need to go outside of the believer to account for our relationship with the truth. Once he makes this move to the outside, the notion of paradox immediately appears as a device for preventing any slippage back to the inside, where a natural point of contact or mediation between ourselves and the truth would once again be introduced. More to the point, this move to the outside, together with the strategy designed to protect its integrity, assures the theological irrelevance of historical knowledge, whether it be merely approximate or not.

As Kierkegaard succinctly puts the matter in the *Postcript*, there can "be no direct transition from the historical to the eternal," from the professor's study to knowledge of God.[17] The characteristic appeal here to the dualism between the temporal and the eternal underwrites the incommensurability between the revelation and its historical manifestation, and also between faith and all forms of knowledge. Within Kierkegaard's scheme, the divine presence in history is protected by something like Kant's noumenal shield; indeed, Kierkegaard's position is thoroughly Kantian. This is why even the most steadfast witness to the incarnation, who has "reduced his hours of sleep to a minimum in order that he might follow this Teacher about, attending him more closely than the pilotfish the shark," and who employed a "hundred spies in his service to watch over the Teacher everywhere," would still not detect the slightest glimmer of the divine.[18] Even less, then, is the divine presence the sort of thing that could be perceived by a later generation through historical reconstruction.

Even at this epistemological level, the parallelism between Kierkegaard's conception of the "moment" of the incarnation and the "moment" of faith is maintained. For just as there is a noumenal shield protecting the Kierkegaardian object of faith, there is a corresponding noumenal shield protecting the inner recesses of this all-important subject of faith, the true disciple. This becomes clear in Kierkegaard's claim that we can never truly "know" or recognize an authentically religious person, the presumptions of Christendom notwithstanding. The Kantian attitude toward the profound concealment of the true moral worth of another person is recapitulated almost exactly in Kierkegaard's idea of the "knight of faith," whose identity remains forever hidden from the scrutiny of others.[19] Lessing and Kant rely on a similar invisibility in order to protect the moral autonomy of the individual; Kierkegaard relies on it to defend the sanctity of the believer's personal relationship with God. Thus, whereas Kierkegaard—in contrast to Lessing and Kant—steps outside of the believer to delineate the truth and proper object of faith, he is at one with them when describing the process of appropriation. In all three cases, the turn toward the private self aids the general strategy of avoiding religious reliance on theoretical inquiry into external, public, factual data. What is private and hidden is religiously preeminent.

In Kierkegaard's case, the noumenal shield protecting the proper object of faith, making it impossible to "see" except through the "eyes of faith," indicates that faith's content is safe from all theoretical intrusions. Consequently, for all their differences, Kierkegaard and Lessing agree that authentic religious faith is immune to the effects of new "information," such as might be provided by ongoing historical and scientific inquiry. Faith simply does not turn on matters of factual information or theoretical data, and this remains true whether the information is potentially damaging or potentially positive and supportive. Consequently, the possibility that the believer might have to keep one eye on the scholarly journals, with the fear that some discovery or new methodology may force an alteration in one's confession of faith, simply never arises.

Alternatively, appeals to historical or scientific evidence as supportive of faith or as providing sufficient grounds for religious assent are grossly inappropriate. Faith is not the measured, deliberative end product of a cautious process of inference that begins with dispassionate examinations of factual and theoretical data. Expressed in a different idiom, faith exists in no relation whatever to external evidence. This severing of the tie between religious assent and sufficient external evidence, already evident before Kant in Lessing, is one of the chief results of the Kantian legacy in religious epistemology, a legacy that has an important representative in Kierkegaard.

The chief lesson here for the entire inquiry is, by now, sufficiently obvious. Kierkegaard's position involves a progression *from* faith *to* the revelatory status of the relevant historical events. Historical knowledge is thus not theologically inadequate because it yields mere approximation knowledge; it is inadequate—or, more properly expressed, simply beside the point—because the object of faith is not a possible object of *any* sort of knowledge, approximate or not. That which is religiously decisive never "appears" phenomenally, and the epistemological consequences of this principle drop into place automatically. As a result, the fact that historical knowledge is always only approximation knowledge cannot gain any purchase on the genuinely theological matters at hand: gradations ("approximations") simply have no point when the issue at stake is dualism. After all, we never find Kant arguing against the value of theoretical knowledge in apprehending the noumenal on the grounds that it yields only "approximation knowledge." Historical knowledge is theologically irrelevant for Kierkegaard, not because it is approximate but because it is knowledge.

Likewise, to be committed to the utter dichotomy between our temporal situation and the eternity of God is to waive the need to adjudicate among various forms of knowing, as though something truly theological were hanging in the balance. Kierkegaard's point is not that historical knowledge *potentially* stands in a positive relation to faith, but in fact does not because of an epistemological shortcoming; he means to show that historical knowledge stands in *no* relation to faith. His only purpose in characterizing historical knowledge at all is to draw attention to the comic disproportion between the subjective passion of faith and the detached viewpoint of the scholar. Consequently, Kierkegaard cannot be fairly appropriated as a corroborating authority figure—or even as a character witness—by those wishing to argue *from* a theory about historical knowledge *to* a conclusion about faith's relation to history. He quite clearly agrees that there is an impasse here, but not because of problems of historical epistemology.

6
Lessing's Ditch and Twentieth-Century Protestant Thought (1)

We ought to be warned against too great or exclusive a preoccupation with [the problem of distance] by the fact that this problem which has become so acute within more recent Protestantism has, all things considered, more the character of a technical difficulty in thinking than that of a spiritual or a genuine theological problem. . . . This does not prevent us from taking the problem of distance with the seriousness proper to it. What it does prevent us from doing is stopping at this discussion, as though it was there that we had to, and could, come to the decision which is necessary.
    —*Karl Barth*, Church Dogmatics, *"The Doctrine of Reconciliation"*

THEOLOGY AND THE PRESUPPOSITIONS
OF HISTORICAL RESEARCH

A guiding theme of this study has been the claim that, by the time both Lessing and Kierkegaard get around to characterizing historical knowledge, all the important things have already been decided. This is the shorthand way of saying that the corrigible character of historical knowledge is, in neither of the two cases, the true source of the impasse between religious faith and historical inquiry.

In a certain sense, twentieth-century Protestant theology has correctly grasped this lesson. Since roughly the time of Schweitzer's *Quest of the Historical Jesus*, prominent continental Protestant thinkers have been noticeably reluctant to tie the fate of theology to the successful recovery of a particular historical detail or fact: the twentieth century is, theologically speaking, interesting as a time during which "facts" have fallen into disrepute. Instead of discussing historical facts or results, theologians now discuss "presuppositions"—which is to say, instead of arguing about this or that detail concerning the life of the historical Jesus, theologians now argue about hermeneutics. Precisely because of the realization that historical research will, *in principle*, yield knowledge that is always fragmentary and subject to change and correction, the theologian now appreciates that the decisive difficulty concerns the divergent sets of presuppositions separating the historian and the believer.

This lesson was underscored early in this century by Ernst Troeltsch and has been repeated more recently by Van Harvey.[1] In his efforts to clarify the principles of secular historical understanding, Troeltsch appreciated that the real problem for theology was not that biblical critics emerged "from their libraries with results disturbing to believers," but that the historical-critical method itself was "based on assumptions quite irreconcilable with traditional belief."[2] The impasse between faith and historical-critical research was not accidental and potentially avoidable, but intrinsic and inevitable. According to Troeltsch, the historian's presuppositions included, for example, the principle of correlation, which requires that all historical events be located in their surrounding historical context and understood in terms of their causal antecedents. As Troeltsch correctly saw, this commonplace historiographical principle has the devastating effect of outlawing *in advance* any claim to absolute or final truth in ethical and religious matters.[3] Moreover, this principle erodes the presumed uniqueness of Christianity by placing it in relation to outside cultural and religious influences, thereby eliminating the possibility of simply calling Christianity true and other religions false.[4] And, by forcing us to understand even religious phenomena—including scripture—in terms of natural processes of cause and effect, the principle of correlation works to squeeze out the idea of divine inspiration as a way of interpreting the Bible. As a result, the traditional orthodox way of affirming the authority of scripture is seriously undermined, if not altogether eliminated. Finally, far from replacing the inspired view of the text with a new way of asserting biblical authority, the principle of correlation promotes the view that biblical claims are simply "relative" to a world view and cultural environment no longer our own.

Likewise, Troeltsch's principle of analogy, which stipulates that we are able to make judgments of historical probability "only if we presuppose that our own present experience is not radically dissimilar to the experience of past persons,"[5] effectively eliminates the category of miracle from historical research. The principle of analogy is the historiographical vindication of Hume: no amount of evidence or testimony for a putative historical event can offset the need for an analogous event in contemporary experience. This principle is also a vindication of the Lessing who noted the important difference between miracles and fulfilled prophecies that he himself experienced and those that history told him others had experienced. In tandem with the principle of correlation, Troeltsch's principle of analogy produces what is perhaps the single most decisive result of modern historical method for an older Protestant orthodoxy— namely, the elimination of supernatural intervention as a possible category of historical explanation.

Troeltsch also isolated what has been called the principle of criticism. This principle is, in effect, the final systematization of the insights present in a characterization of historical knowledge as "accidental" or "merely approximate." In other words, this principle states, at the level of historiographical presuppositions, why historical results will always be corrigible; one does not have to keep testing incoming historical results before making this judgment. Accordingly, the principle of criticism stipulates that we can never classify our claims about the past as being simply "true" or "false," but as only *provisionally* true or false. The epistemological character of historical knowledge dictates that we must always understand such knowledge "as claiming only a greater or lesser degree of probability and as always open to revision."[6] This intrinsic corrigibility means that even the most assured historical claims, eliciting the widest possible consensus among historians, are, in principle at least, falsifiable. Whether or not such assured historical results are ever falsified *in fact* does not affect the basic epistemological issue to which Troeltsch is drawing our attention.

All three of Troeltsch's principles are accurate representations of assumptions that historians, more or less consciously, employ in their work.[7] Moreover, all three principles, suggestive of a fundamental impasse between theology and historical inquiry, properly evoke the image of a ditch or divide between faith and history. Consequently, prominent twentieth-century theologians, sensitive to the lessons taught by Troeltsch, state the problem of faith's relation to historical research in a manner designed to show that it is a problem *in principle*, and not simply because of this or that particular result of actual historical inquiry. Paul Tillich's comment is typical. "Like all historical knowledge," he tells us, "our knowledge of [Jesus] is fragmentary and hypothetical." He continues:

> Historical research subjects this knowledge to hypothetical skepticism and to continuous change in particulars as well as essentials. Its ideal is to reach a high degree of probability, but in many cases this is impossible.[8]

Referring to Martin Kähler's rejection of the theological legitimacy of a quest of the historical Jesus, Tillich adds that one emphasis "in Kähler's answer to the faith-history problem is decisive for our present situation"—that is, "the necessity to make the certainty of faith independent of the unavoidable uncertainties of historical research."[9] Or, as New Testament scholar John Knox puts it, since "even the best attested facts of the history of the past can possess no more than a very high degree of probability," faith can never rest on the acceptance of historical facts. For, says Knox, faith "must *know* its object in a way we cannot know a historical fact."[10] Endorsing this insight at the outset, the theologian will not even attempt to set faith and historical-critical results in a positive correlation, supportive of faith. Because of the antithetical sets of presuppositions, there is simply no point in attempting such a correlation.[11]

Troeltsch himself was destined to become one of those thinkers whose subsequent influence resided largely in the negative or critical side of his work, rather than in the positive or constructive side.[12] Certainly the sociology of German academic theology in the years following World War I had something to do with this. It is of more than passing significance, for example, that the chief leaders of the emerging neo-orthodox or dialectical theology—namely, Barth and Bultmann—were decisively influenced by their teacher, Wilhelm Herrmann, who came from the opposite end of the theological spectrum from Troeltsch.[13] Particularly at the level of christology, some sort of combination of Herrmann, Martin Kähler, and Kierkegaard would exert a profound influence on the new dialectical wing in German Protestantism, as it wrestled with the problem of faith's relation to history—in the shadow, not only of Troeltsch, but of Schweitzer as well. Several years before Kierkegaard was a familiar name to large numbers of theologians, Kähler had exploited the distinction between *Historie* and *Geschichte* in his written response to the life-of-Jesus movement, entitled *The So-Called Historical Jesus and the Historic Biblical Christ.*[14] This distinction would sustain a variety of twentieth-century strategies for successfully relating faith and historical inquiry, supposedly without doing violence to either one.

Likewise, Herrmann's appeal to the "inner life" of Jesus as the true ground of faith, however flawed it was acknowledged to be, suggested a theological method that seemingly insulated faith from the ravages of historical research, without altogether ceasing to be critical.[15] Indeed, as one commentator has suggested, the "central aim" of Herrmann's theology was precisely the "vindication of faith as having a means of winning assurance independently of the shifting results of historical investigation."[16] Bultmann, for one, could never keep from sounding sympathetic even as he criticized the theological standpoint of his former teacher, for he understood that, despite their differences, he and Herrmann shared the same basic aims.[17] The influence, finally, of Kierkegaard, felt especially after 1918, reinforced the tendencies already evident in Kähler and Herrmann, particularly as Kierkegaard's comments about historical knowledge became common coin.[18]

However, even as they fled from the presumed idealism and immanentalism of Troeltsch's several efforts to resolve the historical problem, the exponents of dialectical theology implicitly accepted Troeltsch's way of *posing* the problem. This would at least be true for those who, like Bultmann and Gogarten, kept historical problems at the very center of theology, in contrast to Barth, who somehow remained largely immune to most of the difficulties posed by historical criticism; for Barth had determined early on that proper theology "begins just at the point where the difficulties disclosed by Strauss . . . are seen and then laughed at"[19]—a laughter which, as Robert Morgan has recently reminded us, has not made these difficulties go away.[20] It might be argued, in other words, that thinkers like Herrmann, Kähler, and Kierkegaard appealed to the dialectical wing precisely because they offered a pathway around the problems coming to expression in Troeltsch's historicism: Troeltsch exposed the several ways in which historical criticism was a problem for theology; the others promised the possibility of that "invulnerable area" where faith would be entirely insulated from the troublesome methodological issues raised by historical research.[21]

Certainly, Troeltsch's suspicion that faith and historical method were incompatible in principle, and not incompatible merely because of the results of actual historical research, became normative for much Protestant theology in the years following World War I. The character of historical knowledge as such, and not simply the stock of historical knowledge—be it large or small—that we possess at any one time, was the problem. It was because of the nature of historical knowing that faith and historical research were judged to be incommensurable. Translating this point from a potential deathblow into a theological advantage was simplified by the Luther renaissance of the early years of this century, and thus the renewed importance of the ability to appeal to the authority of Luther when engaging in theological polemics.[22] Bultmann and others like him could claim that their view of the incommensurability between faith and historical research was simply the reformulation—demanded by the new, post-Enlightenment intellectual situation—of the traditional Lutheran principle of justification by faith and not by (intellectual) works.[23] From this standpoint, any attempt to join theology and historical research in a positive correlation was, in effect, to seek to give an illegitimate "prop" to faith.

In this situation, the epistemological precariousness of all historical reconstruction, conveyed especially by Troeltsch's principle of criticism, was not only emphasized but even welcomed. Referring to attempts to support faith through historical research, Bultmann spoke of "salvage operations." "I calmly let the fire burn, for I see that what is consumed is only the fanciful portraits of Life-of-Jesus theology, and that means nothing other than 'Christ after the flesh.' "[24] The full endorsement of such features of historical inquiry as were exposed by Troeltsch's three principles was part of a broader theological effort to show the independence of faith from the labors of the university professor and from the best intellectual products of the culture at large. Kierkegaard's day had arrived.

Consequently, mainstream Protestant theology from roughly 1920 to 1960 proceded on the basis of a kind of double-entry bookkeeping, one column for faith and one column for historiography. In several variations on a fundamentally Kierkegaardian theme, theologians such as Bultmann and Tillich would locate the assurance of faith in a logical space distinct from that occupied by the mere probabilities of historical inquiry. Such a result appears to be the vindication of Troeltsch's perception of the incompatibility, in principle, between theology and the presuppositions of historical research.

Van Harvey summarizes Troeltsch's relationship to modern theology by stressing that, like Troeltsch's other two principles, the principle of criticism raises "the profoundest of questions for faith."

> Barth, Brunner, Bultmann, and Tillich argued, as Martin Kähler and Soren Kierkegaard had done before them, that faith is a passion which becomes comic and distorted if it tries to rest on the "approximation process" of historical inquiry. Faith has, they claimed, its own certitude, and it is a falsification of both faith and historical inquiry if the former is based on the latter: a falsification of faith because faith cannot change with every new consensus of New Testament criticism or hold its breath lest some discovery in the Dead Sea area casts a shadow of doubt over this or that particular belief; falsification of history because it is intolerable to honest inquiry if the New Testament critic or believer decides in favor of one historical judgment rather than another because it is more compatible with his religious beliefs.[25]

Harvey's comment helpfully summarizes a familiar dilemma and implicitly suggests the reasons for the theological appeal of such dichotomies as the "Jesus of history and the Christ of faith," or the *historisch* and the *geschichtlich*. Moreover, Harvey's own *The Historian and the Believer*, with its depiction of a Troeltsch-like impasse in terms of competing "moralities of knowledge,"[26] is among the most clear-headed discussions of the several problems attending the relationship between theology and history in recent years. Yet Harvey's references to both Kierkegaard and the notion of "approximation knowledge," as well as the epistemological-methodological accent conveyed by the idea of a "morality of knowledge," potentially perpetuate a certain confusion, one that applies to Troeltsch as well as to Harvey. The confusion concerns the role played by strictly *factual* difficulties in the impasse between faith and history. Like the principle of analogy, the principle of criticism—the idea that every historical claim attains only a greater or lesser degree of probability—confronts us with a fundamentally factual issue: the force of both principles is to press the question of whether or not a certain reported event really happened. In other words, we have here a recapitulation of what I have been calling the temporal ditch, constituted by chronological distance from religiously momentous historical events.

Understood this way, the problem being pressed by both Troeltsch and Harvey would appear to be the result of our inability to have eyewitness experience of the decisive historical events to which the theologian refers. It is precisely this inability that informs Troeltsch's principle of criticism: the unalterable, intrinsic difference between ourselves and the eyewitness is what makes Troeltsch's principle a *presupposition* of historical inquiry.

The positions of the prominent theologians named by Harvey would not be changed, however, because of eyewitness experience of the relevant historical events, including the incarnation. This is because these thinkers, dominating the dialectical wing of modern Protestant theology, have typically been good Kierkegaardians (and Kantians) when it comes to addressing the relation between history and revelation. In ways that may vary in detail, but which are generically identical to the position put forward in Kierkegaard's Climacus writings, these theologians consistently maintain that God's presence or action in history is never the sort of thing that an eyewitness could "see" or experience in normal empirical terms. Revelation never "appears" phenomenally; underscoring this claim is a crucial aspect of the dialectical theologians' general repudiation of an idealist identification of history and revelation.[27] Whether the decisive historical moment is construed in terms of the arrival of the God-man (Kierkegaard), the occurrence of the "eschatological event" (Bultmann), the appearance of the "New Being" (Tillich), or in some other form, its decisive, revelatory character is always invisible to worldly eyes.

Accordingly, God's saving action occurs "within" history, but it never appears "from the standpoint" of history.[28] Faith's perception always has a "nevertheless" character: it neither reads the religious message directly off of the events of history, as though certain occurrences univocally convey one straightforward religious meaning that any fair and right-minded secular historian would be compelled to admit; nor does faith's perception contradict or in any way encroach upon the activities of the secular historian, promoting an explicitly "religious" view of history that is set in competition with a naturalistic view.[29] As in the case of Kierkegaard's imaginary eyewitness to the incarnation, the person of faith does not see anything different from the normal worldly course of events. This is a crucial side-effect of modern Protestantism's rejection of an outmoded supernaturalism and its openness to historical-critical results, wherever they may lead. More importantly, the theological blindness of historiography is crucial for defending the "divine incognito," rendered in representative form by Bultmann in terms of the principle that "God is not a given entity" of which direct knowledge might be possible.[30] God is always subject and never object. Consequently, to insist on the theological blindness of historiography is, for proponents of this view, not to make a virtue out of necessity; instead, it is to protect the idea of divine sovereignty, while also deepening the insights conveyed by the principle of justification by faith through grace and sustaining the traditionally Protestant preoccupation with the unmediated, highly personal relationship between God and believer.[31]

Obviously, if faith's perception always has a "nevertheless" character—enjoying its integrity *despite* what history shows and not *because of* what history shows—then the factual difficulties posed by the principles of analogy and criticism can hardly be cause for alarm. If being an eyewitness to the relevant historical events carries no religious advantage, then difficulties in historical reconstruction of these events will carry no disadvantage. In this situation, to underscore historiographical difficulties—whether in terms of the results *or* the presuppositions of historical inquiry—would be to reintroduce the red herring present in Lessing's comments about the "accidental truths" of history or in Kierkegaard's comments about "approximation knowledge." In a post-Troeltsch theological environment, the assumption seems to be that a more profound insight is somehow at work when depicting these problems in terms of historiographical presuppositions rather than in terms of actual historical results. But if, in both cases, the net effect is to press the "Did it really happen?" question—in a context where nothing of *theological* importance rides on the answer to this question—then no particular advance or deepening of insight has occurred at all.

If a given theological position stands to gain nothing from the assurances of firsthand eyewitness experience, then such a position cannot lose anything because of the risks and uncertainties intrinsic to historical reconstruction, or because of the fundamental incompatibility between theology and historical method. This lesson remains true whether we are talking about the results or the presuppositions of historical inquiry.

The final irony here is that Troeltsch's principle of criticism, which underscores the intrinsic corrigibility of all historical knowledge, is itself impossible to state in a way that is not self-refuting. That is, even if it were allowed that, in some tangential way, the temporal ditch was theologically germane, reliance on the principle of criticism in the statement of the fundamental problem would be open to serious philosophical objection. By stipulating that all our claims about the past must be judged to be only *provisionally* true or false—because there is always the possibility of future change and correction—the principle of criticism effectively casts doubt on our ability really to "know" a historical claim. One could illustrate the problem by citing the numerous instances in which reputable historians, who once agreed that event E occurred, determined through subsequent discoveries or new historiographical methods that E did not occur in just the assumed manner, or even that E did not occur at all.[32] This obviously means, however, that the historians could not really have *known* that E occurred; instead, they merely *claimed* to know it did, and they turned out to be mistaken. Presumably, historiographical revisions of this sort, ranging widely from modifications of trivial details to major alterations in the historical record, are intrinsic to the genuinely "critical" aspect of modern historical research. It is the historiographical counterpart to the self-correcting feature of natural scientific method.

On the one hand, this problem of corrigibility, brought to our attention by Troeltsch, is of course of fundamental interest and importance to biblical scholarship, regardless of our final determination of its bearing on systematic and dogmatic theology. The corrigibility issue draws our attention to the intimate and important relationship between historical knowledge and other forms of empirical knowledge. This is also a peculiar relationship: on the one hand, historical knowledge is *like* all other forms of empirical knowledge because of its corrigibility and because it always remains subject (at least in principle) to an infinite number of tests and procedures for verification or falsification; yet historical knowledge is *unlike* many other forms of empirical knowledge because of the impossibility, by definition, of experiencing at firsthand the referent of any particular historical claim. In an interesting way, Kierkegaard recognized just this idiosyncrasy, since the "coming into existence" that was for him the decisive predicate of the historical always eludes present experience. We can never really "know" the historical at all, but must always apprehend the historical through an act of will. This is one way of posing the troublesome "past-ness" of history that has made historical knowledge such a conundrum for certain empirically minded philosophers.[33] The problem of truth in historical assertions is here compounded by a more subtle problem of reference, since we always need to ask what it is that our statements concerning the past could possibly be *about*, while simultaneously acknowledging that we can never really know the answer to this question with absolute certainty.[34]

In his depiction of the principle of criticism, then, Troeltsch has placed these and other important difficulties before us. The snag occurs, however, when we attempt to move from the undeniable specific instances of mistakes and inaccuracies in the historical record to the general claim regarding corrigibility that Troeltsch wants to make a presupposition of historical research. For the mere discovery in certain instances—however many—that historians really did not know what they claimed to know cannot be used to substantiate the general principle that *no* claim about the past can be known with conclusive certainty. For if we claim that earlier historians could not really have *known* that event E occurred, but merely thought or claimed they knew it, then we must now know with conclusive certainty that E did *not* in fact occur.[35] The implicit skepticism of this position must, however, be applied fairly. Consequently, if the whole point of this position regarding historical knowledge is that we can never know with absolute certainty any statement about the past, then we can hardly promote such a position by claiming with conclusive certainty that one particular event did not occur. In Peter Carnley's characterization, if "one premise of the argument assumes that the falsity of an historical statement can be conclusively established, it cannot be employed to prove the general argument that *no* statement about the past can be conclusively established."[36] Proponents of this form of historical skepticism fail to recognize that the sword in their hands is double-edged: it cuts against their own argument as much as it damages the search for certainty in matters of historical inquiry. In effect, efforts to spell out the consequences of Troeltsch's principle of criticism suffer problems analogous to those affecting formulations of historical relativism. The position apparently cannot be stated without making of itself an exception to its own rule.

Again, if we discover that the problem of the temporal ditch is simply irrelevant to the theological position in question, then the full cluster of issues related to the corrigibility problem ceases to be germane. My point here is mainly to suggest several reasons for concluding that Troeltsch's "shadow" is not as threatening to modern theology as it is often presumed to be. With specific respect to the principle of criticism, there remains a fundamentally philosophical reason for revising Troeltsch's definition of the problem of relating theology to historical inquiry. This concerns the role played by the contingency-necessity distinction in Troeltsch's depiction of the corrigibility of all historical knowledge. Like Lessing and Kierkegaard before him, Troeltsch is saying that historical knowledge is always "contingent." Its accidental or contingent character means that historical knowledge could, in principle, always be something other than what it is. This is the whole point of corrigibility.

But contingency only makes sense in a philosophical context where logical necessity also resides. However unproblematic this assumption was for Troeltsch—and for Lessing and Kierkegaard as well—assuming the validity of the contingency-necessity distinction has ceased to be an unspoken matter of course. Instead, the distinction is at the very center of recent debates about just what sort of field philosophy is and, more specifically, about the need to reevaluate the fundamentally Cartesian categories and dualisms that have provided the "givens" in modern philosophical debate and argument. The specific issue concerns the attack on the notion of logical necessity, an attack arising out of the work of the later Wittgenstein and such contemporary philosophers as Willard van Ormen Quine, Wilfrid Sellars, and Richard Rorty. As evidenced by Quine's specific attack on the analytic-synthetic distinction,[37] all of these thinkers are suspicious of any notion of necessity other than that which we arrive at through the conventions of our social life and discourse. The very idea of necessity arises out of the demands of practice; in other words, our views of necessary truth are dependent on something that is not itself necessary. So-called necessary or logical truths simply happen to occupy a particularly fixed location in our linguistic space. Yet what *counts* as necessary may change, depending upon the evolving demands of practice. As Rorty summarizes the matter, "whereas once we thought, with Aristotle, that necessity came from things, and later thought with Kant that it came from the structure of our minds, we now know that it comes from language."[38]

This is hardly the place to sort out the issue in a highly technical philosophical debate.[39] All I wish to do here is to draw attention to the possibility that the idea of necessary truth may be going the way of phlogiston—which means, among other things, that the idea of *contingency* loses its contrast case. If this happens, then every Troeltsch-like effort to frame the general question of faith's relation to historical method in terms of the corrigibility of all historical knowledge will have to be revised. Again, if the merely probable and always corrigible character of historical knowledge is portrayed in a manner that draws off of its accidental, "contingent" nature, then no particular advance or improvement has occurred if we pose the issue in terms of the presuppositions, rather than results, of historical inquiry. If the contingency-necessity distinction falls through, then *every* argument for the incommensurability between theology and historical research that relies on the appeal to the contingent, and thus intrinsically corrigible, character of historical knowledge is open to question. The most intriguing point lurking in the pragmatic or conventionalist account of necessity is that the relevant contrast case, implicit whenever historical knowledge is portrayed as having certain epistemological liabilities, is itself subject to those same liabilities. There is really no true dualism here, warranting the idea of a ditch, but simply one continuous epistemological scale—a plain, not a ditch.

Lessing and Kierkegaard have been telling us all along that the problem of relating faith or theology to history is not due to the merely probable or approximate character of historical knowledge. If this were the primary difficulty, then the problem of faith and history would turn out to be fundamentally a factual problem. But the problem, as we have seen, goes far deeper than this. I began this chapter by saying that, "in a certain sense," twentieth-century Protestant theology has grasped this lesson. This account of Troeltsch, however, suggests the force of my earlier qualifying phrase. In a very real sense, the red herring introduced whenever undue empha-

sis falls on the corrigible character of historical knowledge has been
covertly smuggled into the twentieth century by Troeltsch's theory
about the presuppositions of historical research. For all the talk
about the more fundamental dilemma introduced by the discovery
that theology and historical method are incompatible in principle,
and not simply at the level of the negative results of historical research, the effect is still to keep our attention focused on factual
difficulties. If Lessing and Kierkegaard have been proper guides,
however, discussions of factual issues, no matter how sophisticated,
can never fully engage the gears of the decisive theological issues. If,
as both Lessing and Kierkegaard would have it, the fundamental
issue is that of historical revelation and the relation between religious truth and natural modes of human wisdom or insight, then
the adjudication of factual matters will be of little benefit.

HISTORICAL EVENTS AND UNIVERSAL TRUTHS

Alone among Troeltsch's principles of historical research, the principle of correlation raises substantive issues that take us beyond
the temporal ditch. This principle signals the troublesome problem of moving from a stream of historical events, viewed contex-
tually in terms of the surrounding historical and cultural environment, to a universal or soteriologically decisive truth claim. This
is not the temporal ditch, represented by our distance from the
eyewitness; it is the metaphysical ditch, represented especially by
the odd conceptual linkage between historical event and christological claim.

   There is perhaps something vaguely passé about discussions of
Bultmann, Tillich, and other theologians of their era on the problems of faith and history. The same cannot be said about the issues
represented by this metaphysical difficulty. It may in fact be the
case that no small amount of the confusion and sterility of much
recent Protestant thought—or at least much of its technical, in-
house character—has been produced by too much discussion of the
wrong ditch, an overly prolonged attempt to discover "the" technical solution to the problem of faith's relation to historical criticism.
As the preceding accounts of both Lessing and Kierkegaard have
indicated, this issue is clearly distinct from the metaphysical difficulty at stake in all efforts to relate the discrete moments of history
to religious truth or christological claims: having a position on the
relation between religious truth and historical events is materially

different from having a position on the relation between religious truth and historical knowledge.

The chief form in which the metaphysical issue makes its presence felt in more recent theology, both Protestant and Roman Catholic, is in discussions of the relationship between Christian truth claims and natural, secular canons of truth that are, in one sense or another, universally available.[40] This general problem becomes most pressing in connection with christology, since the ultimate question in these matters is that of whether or not a reference to Jesus is required in order to make a Christian truth claim—the question, that is, of whether the appearance of Jesus involves "an absolutely new message dropped in from above," or "simply the spelling out of what the world and mankind already are."[41] Here, the fundamental issue has been defined, not by Troeltsch's principles of historical research, but by Kierkegaard's project of thought. The christological issue raised by that project is intimately related to the further question of whether or not "faith" is simply the discovery, recapitulation, or representation of something we already carry as a natural part of our human inventory, as Lessing supposed and Kierkegaard denied: whereas Lessing draws on a theory of inner truth to show that the lessons of history are at one with natural human insight, Kierkegaard stresses the decisiveness of an indispensable historical moment for both faith and salvation, a moment that can exist only in a paradoxical relationship with natural modes of human reason or insight.

To promote Lessing's position in a contemporary setting would thus require addressing the issue of historical revelation in a manner designed to expose the coincidence between the real or "inner" content of revelation and a given cluster of general truths, arrived at through some combination of metaphysics and philosophical anthropology. The historical particularity of Jesus, and these wider, nonparticular canons of truth, are correlated in a way that effectively subordinates the former to the latter. What comes to expression in the unique moments *of* history—even in the life and career of Jesus—is interpreted and transformed in terms of what the believer innately brings *to* history. This position thus has the potential capacity to reveal the latent yet material connections between Christianity and other religions, in a manner reminiscent of the project in religious tolerance represented by Lessing's *Nathan the Wise*. Moreover, the exposed congruence between natural human insight and the content of revelation typically involves a greatly reduced emphasis on the christological themes of redemption and atonement, and the abandonment altogether of supernaturalist categories of causation and explanation. A significant result of this strategy would invariably be the attenuation or outright severing of the traditional tie to Chalcedonian formulations of the "two natures" doctrine concerning the person of Jesus. There is no need to espouse anything more than the full manhood of Jesus.

Alternatively, those following Kierkegaard will insist on a hiatus between historical revelation and general structures of human experience or insight, just as Kierkegaard separates history from philosophical necessity. The emphasis here falls on history in its "eventful" character: historical revelation makes a genuinely ontological difference to faith and salvation, and is not simply an epistemological helpmate. The resulting accent on the "particularity" of the historical, even though it may be a philosophical scandal, must be preserved at all costs, for otherwise the themes of divine sovereignty and grace are presumably robbed of their meaning. This accent on revelation as an "event" rather than as an illustration of general truths is thus correlated with a low anthropology and an emphasis on motifs of atonement and redemption. Jesus is not accidentally or incidentally related to soteriology, in a manner that can be illuminated metaphysically. He is instead somehow constitutive *of* salvation. Likewise, Jesus is not merely illustrative of a deeper truth, nor does he somehow recapitulate, decode, or coincide with truths that we can arrive at independently of reference to him. Instead, his historical appearance, precisely in its "eventful" character, is itself the theological point: there are no wider categories from which to address this historical event. This Kierkegaardian position may or may not involve a supernaturalist commitment. It is, however, in more obvious continuity than is Lessing's position with Chalcedon's two natures doctrine, although what it gains here in terms of continuity with tradition is perhaps offset by the intellectual difficulties it faces before a modern audience. As in the case of Kierkegaard himself, however, this potential problem of plausibility is perhaps mitigated by the initial assumption that the content of revelation is not continuous with innate powers of human insight anyway. The moral of Kierkegaard's project of thought, after all, is that Christ is an "offense," and faith itself a "paradox."

In large part, Protestant thought in this century has been a series of attempts to mediate some sort of truce between the competing demands represented by these alternative views on history and revelation.[42] Pushing too far in Lessing's direction ultimately leads to a sole emphasis on general revelation, a strong endorsement of natural theology, and, perhaps, the eventual transformation of a distinctively Christian theology into a general philosophy of religion. To push too far in Kierkegaard's direction, however, leads to what has been called a "positivism of revelation," a theology so discontinuous with publically available canons of truth and intelligibility as to be unable to give a convincing account of itself. Stigmatized in this way by Dietrich Bonhoeffer, an extreme of this position "says in effect, Take it or leave it (*Iss, Vogel, oder stirb*): Virgin Birth, Trinity, or anything else, are all equally significant and necessary parts of the whole, which has to be swallowed as a whole or not at all."[43]

But "pure" forms of the two positions—approximated, perhaps, by Henry Nelson Wieman on the one side and by one of the several Karl Barth's on the other—are hard to come by. The bulk of the theological action in our century has been in connection with mediation efforts, whether or not the theologians involved thought of themselves as mediators.

This lesson is perhaps particularly evident in the work of Bultmann and the diverse discussions elicited by his theology. It is well known that, throughout his career, Bultmann was a lightning rod for discussions of Christian faith and historical knowledge. It is just as true to say that his work has both included and evoked considerable discussion of the theme of Christian faith and general truths, even though the discussants themselves might not have acknowledged—or even fully realized—that this theme was ultimately at stake.[44] In light of Bultmann's very explicit employment of Heidegger's philosophy in his account of faith and Christian existence, it was inevitable that the question of general truths should become a focal point of discussions of his work. Critics to the "right" of Bultmann would claim that his existentialist conception of faith finally dissolves into a mere anthropology that ultimately effects a crippling reductionism on all of his efforts to speak meaningfully of God. Critics to Bultmann's "left," on the other hand—many of whom pay homage to him as the source of their own theological inspiration—accuse him of a failure of nerve in his deployment of existentialist hermeneutics, a failure that is most evident in Bultmann's insistence on retaining the reference to an "act of God" in the cross of Jesus.[45]

Debates on these matters became a kind of industry in the middle third of this century. Moreover, such debates usually occurred on a highly technical level in the idiom of a difficult philosophical conceptuality, the difficulty typically compounded by the ways in which a German Lutheran ethos shaped the debates in powerful but unspoken ways. The figure of Bultmann is ceasing to be a central part of ongoing, constructive Protestant theology and is gradually becoming a telling symptom of theology's location within the culture: one does not turn to him to find out what to do next, so much as to discover clues concerning how we landed in the current puzzling situation. All of these factors contribute to the serious category confusions characteristic of many of the discussions associated with Bultmann's name, confusions that invariably involve Lessing's several ditches.

A good example of this sort of confusion is the debate over what some have called the "structural inconsistency" in Bultmann's demythologizing project.[46] This issue, drawing considerable attention in the 1950s and 1960s, concerns precisely the problem of the relation between Christian faith and general truths, but is often addressed as though a methodological issue—an "inconsistency"—is primarily at stake. Thus, the critic ends up accusing Bultmann of a methodological flaw which may actually be the natural expression of a deeply held theological commitment which has to be addressed on a different level than that of methodology. In the process, the theological commitment is made to seem the unfortunate result of a lapse into inconsistency when, in fact, the methodological move (lapse or not) is the by-product of the theological commitment. The result is a debate over the wrong issue, in tandem with an incorrect definition of the options facing the observer of the debate.

Getting clear about this sort of confusion requires some reminders regarding Bultmann's conception of faith. With the help of a Heideggerian conceptuality, Bultmann renders Christian faith in terms of the existentialist category of self-understanding, which he contrasts with an older, more traditional view of faith that associates faith with certain identifiable "beliefs" about history or the cosmos.[47] Faith, according to Bultmann's existentialist view, is not a matter of believing certain propositions that might conflict with scientific and historical inquiry, but is instead the fresh understanding of myself as sinful before God and tied to a fallen past, yet simultaneously justified by God and, through resolve and responsible decision, thereby open to the future in true Christian freedom. Faith, in other words, is nonpropositional: it is an existential *act* of the whole self, and not a static body of beliefs. These existentialist variations on Lutheran themes are, for Bultmann, already latent in the New Testament message itself, particularly in John's gospel and in the letters of Paul. All that is needed, then, is a hermeneutical

device designed to tease out the understanding of Christian existence lurking within the mythological trappings of the New Testament. Bultmann's own program of demythologizing is designed to
fill this need.

Bultmann's existentialist conception of faith, with its radical reduction of the assertorial content within the Christian confession,
suggests for some of his followers that faith can be *exhaustively* interpreted "as man's original possibility of authentic historical (*geschichtlich*) existence as this is more or less adequately clarified and
conceptualized by an appropriate philosophical analysis."[48] In other
words, faith—or authentic existence, which becomes synonymous
with faith in this context—is everywhere and always a human possibility, and is not logically dependent upon any particular historical
event or sequence of events. For someone such as Schubert Ogden,
this follows naturally from Bultman's assumption

> that what is at stake in the Christian message is completely indepen-
> dent of the objective truth or falsity of the mythological assertions in
> which the New Testament authors explicate their faith. This he can do
> because he also takes for granted that the Christian faith is nothing
> other than a possibility of *existentiell* self-understanding, which is
> something entirely different from objective knowledge and assertion.

The snag, however, at least from the standpoint of Ogden and
other critics, is that Bultmann links this rendering of faith in terms
of a general anthropological possibility with reference to an indispensable historical event. As Bultmann himself makes very clear,
the cross-resurrection sequence is for him the decisive "act of God"
that is, in utterly paradoxical fashion, both historical event and
eschatological event. From Bultmann's standpoint, it is only
through this act of God that authentic existence becomes a possibility *in fact* and does not merely remain a possibility in principle.[49] In
other words, existentialist philosophy may accurately conceptualize
authentic existence, but only the act of God can actually effect it.
Because of this deep theological stake—which he identifies with the
Lutheran *sola fide*—Bultmann is unwilling to demythologize the notion of an act of God, insisting instead that to speak of such an act is
to speak analogically and not mythologically.[50] However murky his
trading on this distinction may be, Bultmann's chief claim here is
clear: it is the "eventful" character of historical revelation that gives
faith its point. In this manner, as in many other ways, Bultmann
follows in the tradition of Kierkegaard.

The net effect of Bultmann's position is to retain the reference to a historical event as determinative of faith, in much the same manner of Kierkegaard's project of thought. Ogden and others criticize the apparent inconsistency of retaining this crucial reference to a past event while simultaneously embracing a theory of faith that appears to make faith a universal possibility simply given with the human situation. The universally available existentialist conception of faith appears to be in radical tension with the indispensable reference to Jesus. Hence we have the idea of a "structural inconsistency." Ogden, for one, maintains that the real annoyance is that Bultmann has in fact failed to follow through to its obvious and appropriate conclusion his own correct insight into the nature of faith. The result, supposedly, is that Bultmann ends up in an unsatisfactory halfway house because, at the crucial moment, he unaccountably indulges an unwarranted loyalty to an outmoded christological formulation. However, Ogden and others think that if demythologizing is to be applied at all, it must be applied to traditional language about divine activity, such as the presumed "act of God" in the cross-resurrection sequence.

Thus, debates on these matters proceed as though the decisive questions concern the correct definition of "myth," the relation between speaking mythologically and speaking analogically, and the rigor and consistency with which demythologizing as a hermeneutical strategy is to be carried out. The deeper *theological* question—namely, the question of whether or not Christian faith is dependent for its truth and its meaning upon the reference to a past event—is subtly given second-class status. What is theologically decisive for Bultmann is thus made to appear to be the function of a methodological-hermeneutical decision. That is, the debate proceeds as though, once Bultmann appreciates his methodological inconsistency, he will be forced to admit the inadequacy of his view of the relationship between historical events and general anthropological truths—a shift in theological commitments will follow naturally from a methodological alteration.

The minimum result of such a situation is to generate too much discussion of the wrong issues. A more radical, yet potential, result is to leave the methodological tail wagging the theological dog. One need not actually endorse Bultmann's emphasis on a once-for-all act of God in history in order to appreciate that this emphasis is for him neither the function of, nor subject to, the accidents of methodology. Indeed, it is precisely in order to *get at* the act of God—which, in contrast to virgin births and dead men rising, is for

Bultmann the real stumbling block of Christian faith—that he un-
dertakes demythologizing at all.[51] To suggest that Bultmann should
alter his views on the relation between revelation and history, subsequent to correcting an inconsistency in his theology, would be like
suggesting that Kierkegaard adopt the Socratic viewpoint upon discovering that his own viewpoint ends up in paradox.

The reference to paradox here perhaps suggests where a discussion of these matters should focus. As Jeffrey Stout has recently
said, theologians "determine their relationship to the culture, now
as in Tertullian's day, largely by saying what they say about paradox."[52] The decisive issue separating Ogden and Bultmann is not
"consistency" with respect to demythologizing, but the relationship
between natural human wisdom and Christian truth claims. Continuity between the two eliminates the need for the language of paradox. Historical events, far from being intellectual scandals, are do-
mesticated in terms of the overarching metaphysical viewpoint
providing for this continuity. As a result, the very distinctiveness of
the adjective *Christian* potentially falls through.[53]

Discontinuity between natural human wisdom and Christian
truth claims, however, leads directly to the language of paradox in
the expression of faith. Likewise, the "eventful" character of revelation must be stressed to account for how a humanity, unable to save
itself through its own resources, comes into contact with saving
truth.

To be sure, it is far from clear how we are to decide where to come
down on this issue. It is like asking whether one wants to join the
Socratic or the non-Socratic side in Kierkegaard's project of thought.
Or, biblically expressed, it is like asking for the definitive interpretation of the first chapter of Paul's letter to the Romans. My point here,
however, is simply to suggest where a certain important theological
conversation ought to focus, and not to suggest that the resolution of
these matters can be straightforward. What *is* clear here is that, with
respect to the theological issue I am pinponting, a thinker will not
switch sides because of the sort of methodological difficulty underscored by Ogden. For such a switch as this, the relevant convictions
will presumably run much deeper, as reflected in Bultmann's own
response to Ogden: "I must ask Ogden whether what he calls the
inconsistency of my proposal is not rather the legitimate and necessary character of what the New Testament calls the stumbling
block?"[54]

The true difference between Ogden and Bultmann—like that separating Lessing and Kierkegaard—thus concerns the degree of "scan-

dal" each is willing to tolerate as part of the price of faith. This again is a way of saying that the difference turns on one's attitude toward the relationship between Christian faith and general truths, something that becomes clear in connection with the relationship between christology and revelation. Ogden fairly draws out the christological implication present in his criticism of Bultmann's putative inconsistency. Christian faith, understood in existentialist terms as authentic existence, is possible for Ogden both in principle *and* in fact apart from reference to Jesus.[55] In other words, "faith is by no means completely contingent on a particular historical event." We are once again within the Socratic framework of Kierkegaard's project of thought. For Ogden, the "specific possibility of faith in Jesus Christ is one and the same with a general ontological possibility belonging to man simply as such." Properly construed, christology does not orient us toward a historical event that is uniquely decisive *as* event. Instead, christology illuminates the way Jesus is re-presentative of a truth not tied solely to his historical appearance. The New Testament, for Ogden, "does *not* affirm that in Christ our salvation 'becomes possible.' It affirms, rather, that in him what has always been possible now 'becomes manifest.' " Jesus may provide the "norm" for theological claims, a norm that helps us to assess the truth and adequacy of other theological claims; but he is not the indispensable source of the very possibility of faith and theology. For the "New Testament sense of the claim 'only in Jesus Christ' "

> is not that God is only to be found in Jesus and nowhere else, but that the only God who is to be found anywhere—*though he is to be found everywhere*—is the God who is made known in the word that Jesus speaks and is.

Ogden's point, in a modern recapitulation of Lessing's position, is that the revelation in Jesus may be special, but it is not unique. "Not only is there no other light shining in Jesus than has always already shined in the creation, but no saving act of God occurs in him other than that which never fails to occur as soon and as long as there is any distinctively human being."[56] Ogden contends that the New Testament witness itself emphasizes the grace of God as *creator* over against the grace of God as *redeemer*, leading him toward a revaluation of such traditional categories as nature and grace, as well as toward the subordination of special revelation to general revelation.[57] The special revelation in Jesus may appropriately be called "decisive," but primarily in the sense that it is through reference to Jesus that the specifically Christian community originally fashioned itself and now perpetuates itself as the Christian church.[58] Special revelation is not decisive in the sense that something occurs or comes to expression there that occurs nowhere else.

Consequently, with Kierkegaard's project of thought very much in mind, Ogden contrasts the Socratic understanding, "according to which *no* event is constitutive of man's authentic possibility, because he already possesses it implicitly prior to any event," with Kierkegaard's own understanding, "according to which *some* event is thus constitutive." Against these Ogden poses "a third understanding, according to which *every* event is constitutive of man's possibility,"

> because, while it is in no way his eternal possession, it is given to him at least implicitly in every event that is constitutive of his existence.[59]

It is not altogether clear what the material difference is between saying that no event is decisive for our attaining truth or authenticity, and saying that every event is. Presumably, Ogden emphasizes the supposed difference, not in order to distance himself from the Socratic scheme and draw closer to the Kierkegaardian (and Bultmannian), but in order to jettison the static anthropology of traditional rationalism and to do justice to an expressly existentialist anthropology during reflection on revelation and faith. Certainly, in light of Ogden's demythologization of Bultmann's "act of God" language and his insistence on some sort of continuity between Christian faith and a general anthropology, he is closer to Lessing's position than to Kierkegaard's.

The parallel with Lessing is further illustrated by the linkage in Ogden's thought between an emphasis on general revelation and the "implicit faith" that is for Ogden constitutive of modern secular culture as such.[60] The possibility that faith, as authentic existence, is logically possible apart from reference to Jesus dovetails with Ogden's view that we cannot believe in the meaningfulness of human existence without also believing in God. This remains true even for those who expressly think of themselves as atheists.[61] Thus, in a manner reminiscent not merely of Lessing but of Schleiermacher as well, Ogden posits a connection between general revelation and human nature, a connection that eliminates the theological need for any particular event in history and that transforms christology into the specific articulation of something knowable at all times and in all places. Moreover, this linkage between revelation and human nature automatically solves the problem of religious appropriation, since nothing is ever revealed in history that is not already latent in human consciousness—like Lessing and Schleiermacher, Ogden enjoys the advantages of the "anthropological vestibule" that renders potentially strange or alien aspects of the Christian message in terms dictated by the receiving consciousness. Ogden admits as much with typical bluntness: "If to be a Christian means to say yes where I otherwise say no, or where I do not have the right to say anything at all, then my only choice is to refuse to be a Christian."[62]

Ogden comes far closer in this comment than in his discussion of Bultmann's "structural inconsistency" to locating the true difference between himself and Bultmann. Bultmann is hospitable toward Kierkegaardian language about paradox because faith, for him, is ultimately oriented toward a soteriologically decisive event that is, in dialectical fashion, simultaneously historical and eschatological. A modern philosophical conceptuality—specifically, the existentialism of Heidegger's *Being and Time*—can go a long way toward explicating faith, but it can neither account for faith's occurrence nor set the decisive act of God within an intelligible, overarching pattern. In Ogden's case, on the other hand, anthropological "givens" dictate the boundaries of theological discourse. To insist otherwise would be to force Ogden "to refuse to be a Christian." The difference between these two theologians is not a function of the degree to which each is willing to demythologize; the degree to which each is willing to demythologize is a function of a difference at the more fundamental level that is captured in Kierkegaard's project of thought. The chief issue here is not methodological at all, but involves instead the question of the potential uniqueness of what comes to expression in Jesus. The chief issue, in other words, is Lessing's metaphysical ditch and the problem of relating a religious truth claim to a historical event.

7
Lessing's Ditch and Twentieth-Century Protestant Thought (2)

Is it not the case that it is not primarily its historical distance and singularity but its own nature which makes this event a riddle, a kind of erratic block in our sphere and time and space?
—*Karl Barth*, Church Dogmatics, *"The Doctrine of Reconciliation"*

THE KANTIAN CONTEXT OF MODERN PROTESTANT REFLECTION ON THEOLOGY AND HISTORY

Bultmann's emphasis on a paradoxically unique historical event, and the existentialist anthropology of both Bultmann and Ogden, are symptoms of Kierkegaard's substantial legacy to twentieth-century Protestant thought. It is at least arguable that, in the words of one commentator, "Protestant theology since Kierkegaard has tended to accept his distinctions as normative."[1] Certainly Kierkegaard's influence is clearly evident whenever there is a strict divorce between historical "facts" and Christian faith. As we have seen, this divorce turns on exploiting the difference between what is public and open to empirical scrutiny, and what is private and hidden from worldly eyes. The profound hiddenness of both revelation and faith depends entirely on this distinction. Consequently, potentially disturbing factual questions are put to rest, not by satisfactorily answering them but by switching the scene of religious action from the outer, public world to the private, religious self. In his appeal to the "inner truth" of authentic religion, Lessing, as we have seen, is a kind of precursor to this switch. But only in a post-Kantian atmosphere could the switch become complete, as it does with Kierkegaard.

Modern theology is still arguing the wisdom of this Kierkegaardian move, particularly in debates concerning the topics of subjectivity and objectivity. Philosophically considered, at issue here is not simply Kierkegaard's legacy to Protestant theology, but the legacies of Kant and, finally, Descartes as well.[2] Theologically considered, the ultimate question is perhaps the extent to which Christian faith "refers" to something other than to the religious consciousness. This question arises quite naturally and inevitably, not only in the wake of Schleiermacher on the one hand and of Feuerbach on the other, but also subsequent to the stilling of historical-critical difficulties through appeal to the dynamics of religious appropriation. The emphasis on appropriation—as the examples of Kierkegaard and his existentialist successors clearly show—requires an ever more sophisticated theory of the religious self, a theory about what it is that triggers or makes possible our apprehension of the religious message, in light of the fact that this apprehension is no longer a matter of assent to historical propositions. How one describes the process of religious appropriation will thus be largely a function of what one takes the self to be.[3]

The dialectical theology emerging in the years following World War I clearly exhibits the dual Kierkegaardian appeal to a decisive historical event and to a present-day faith that is both profoundly private and immune to the effects of historical research. The early Barth, Gogarten, Tillich, and Bultmann all shared a fresh sense of the vitalities of faith, together with a view of the Bible that effectively emptied historical research of any theological value.[4] This general development helps to explain why, for Continental Protestantism in particular, the decisive theological discipline has gradually become hermeneutics. Nineteenth-century interest in historical "facts" gives way to existentialist conceptions of faith and increasingly sophisticated views of the conditions for understanding or appropriating the biblical message. In this situation, standard historical research may well proceed, but not for theological reasons.

More than one commentator has noted that the emerging notions of faith, selfhood, and appropriation gradually put into question faith's need to refer to a decisive historical event at all.[5] That is, the anthropological conceptuality making faith independent of historical results may also sever the connection between faith and an indispensable historical event—even among those who, unlike Ogden, insist on retaining the indispensable reference to the past. This severing occurs because the logic involved in freeing faith from historical knowledge may implicitly reveal that faith is, in some sense, an anthropological "given," independent of any particular historical referent. The rationale for freeing faith from dependence on historical *facts* mischievously contains the seeds of a rationale for freeing faith from particular historical *events* as well. In large measure, it is this insight that informs Ogden's response to Bultmann.

The issue here ultimately concerns the balancing act between an-

thropology and theology that has to be performed in a post-Kantian
atmosphere, where straightforward and unproblematic references to
God or divine action are an impossibility. It is a question, in other
words, of how to be "dialectical." A considerable measure of Karl
Barth's genius lies in the way he grasped the subtlety of this difficulty and altered the fundamentally Kierkegaardian course he had
set for himself in his *Römerbrief*.[6] Looking back on his earlier, Kierkegaardian self, Barth asked whether "a new anthropocentric sys-
tem" did not

> announce itself in Kierkegaard's theoretical groundwork—one quite
> opposed to that at which we aimed? . . . a theology oriented towards
> and subsisting essentially on Kierkegaard was possible only where
> Schleiermacher had not been read with sufficient care and one had not
> been warned definitely against a continuation of this programme, in-
> cluding an existential one.[7]

The question is whether an orientation toward the religious self,
mandated by the insistence that Christian faith is not the result of
assent to historical facts, might not have a reductionistic effect on
theology. As attractive as Kierkegaard was to Barth hermeneuti-
cally, especially in a theological setting defined by the signers of the
declaration supporting the Kaiser's war, there was the distinct possibility that his path, like Schleiermacher's, led to an anthropological captivity of theology. Barth's nervousness about reductionism,
and his keen sense that there were several ways to fall into Feuerbach's trap, thus induced his break with an existentialist conceptuality and his ultimately sharp criticisms of one-time allies such as
Gogarten and Bultmann.[8]

At stake here is not so much the merit of Barth's position as the
question he raises. Kierkegaardian independence from historical inquiry subtly merges with serious difficulties concerning the content
of faith and the very possibility of theology. Appeal to an inflated or
exaggerated notion of the subject of faith introduces new difficulties, even as it puts to rest the old difficulties potentially posed by
historical criticism. The specter of Troeltsch is avoided, but only to
be replaced by the specter of Feuerbach.

These problems, particularly pressing when seen in connection
with those thinkers (such as Bultmann) who rigorously developed
an existentialist conceptuality for theology, are perhaps simply the
result of the emergence of a noumenal, Kantian self to a position of
prominence in modern Protestant conceptions of faith. The capacity

of a Kantian self to be more than purely self-reflexive has been a
question mark for Western thought ever since Kant's own theory of
the unity of apperception and the transition from Kantian transcen-
dentalism to early idealism.[9] Post-Kantian theology thus faces a peculiar variation on the Reformation debate over the relative balance
between the *pro me* and the *extra me* in the economy of faith. The
debate hangs on properly mediating the competing tendencies, evident in Luther himself, to think personalistically in connection with
anthropology, but ontologically in connection with God, or "theology" itself.[10] During the past two centuries, this has become the
much more complex problem of thinking through the Lutheran *pro
me* in the accounting of faith, subsequent to the virtual amputation
of the *pro me* from its dogmatic, propositional basis brought about
by Kant's critical philosophy and by historical criticism.[11] Kierkegaard himself is squarely in the tradition—extending from Kant
through Ritschl and Herrmann to Bultmann, and such post-Bult-
mannians as Fritz Buri—for which the Lutheran *pro me* effectively
introduces a gulf "between dogmatic, ontological, historical statements and personalistic, existential statements."[12] Establishing a
corridor between the two, in a way that suggests their interrelation-
ship, invariably involves putting theology at the mercy of either a
general metaphysics, on the one hand, or historical criticism, on the
other.

Whatever its merits, Barth's polemic against "anthropocentric"
theology at least pinpoints the decisive issue often lurking beneath
the surface of debates about other matters. Moreover, pressing the
problem of the reference and content of faith reintroduces the question Kierkegaard himself was *not* interested in—namely, the question concerning the "what" of Christianity. When leading theologians are characterized as giving the culture "less and less in which
to disbelieve" as they execute their chosen tasks,[13] and when it is
suggested that theologians have avoided historical-critical and other
cognitive difficulties only by evacuating Christian belief "of all its
traditional content,"[14] then the "what" question ceases to be a matter of indifference. On the answer to this question hangs the answer
to whether or not Christian faith really *asserts* anything. After all, it
seems fair to suggest that if faith asserts nothing—if faith has nothing whatever to do with possible states of affairs, preeminent among
them the metaphysical actuality of God—then it is simply not clear
what conceivable difference it might make to call oneself a Christian. A view of faith that empties it of all assertorial content permits
the *form* of Christian discourse to survive, and, indeed, to survive

quite nicely in dialogue with the general culture.[15] But perhaps this survival is purchased only by robbing Christian discourse of its distinctiveness.[16]

It is in the context of such issues as these that the theology of Wolfhart Pannenberg ceases to appear merely as a strange aberration from Kantian norms and becomes instead a telling symptom of something important. Pannenberg is one of those figures who is too outlandish to elicit widespread agreement, but too perceptive in his critique of accepted fashions to be ignored. Like Barth—but for radically different reasons—Pannenberg is suspicious of the subjectivizing tendencies evident in modern theological reactions to problems posed by history and historical research. He is not simply rejecting certain details characteristic of such thinkers as Bultmann and his followers; he is repudiating the entire Kantian-Kierkegaardian legacy within modern German Protestantism. This is what lies behind the most distinctive—and, for our purposes, most interesting— feature of Pannenberg's theology, something that makes it highly illuminating to draw him into this discussion as a contrast case to everything that has gone before. This key feature of his thought is the positive correlation that Pannenberg posits between theology and historical inquiry. Indeed, in stark contrast to the traditions of both Lessing and Kierkegaard, Pannenberg insists upon grounding Christian faith in the results of historical research.

A series of important reversals must obviously be taking place within such a viewpoint as this. And it should be said at the outset that the entire, interlocking grid of issues exposed by the present inquiry must be kept in view if one-sided interpretations and facile criticisms of Pannenberg are to be avoided. Pannenberg maintains that the Protestant reformers, Luther included, never intended their emphasis on faith as *fiducia* to be cut loose from the elements of *notitia* and *assensus* in the accounting of faith.[17] Yet Pannenberg sees just this divorce or separation occurring within modern theological attempts to insulate faith from historical research. He is focusing here on the familiar distinction between faith as "belief that" and faith as "belief in," and suggesting that the former has been lost from view while increasingly sophisticated and complex versions of the latter have been invoked as a means of overcoming historical-critical difficulties.

But, insists Pannenberg, faith or trust *in* something must logically presuppose faith or belief *that* something is the case. Even as a personal sense of trust or assurance—a Protestant motif that Pannenberg has no wish to repudiate, only rehabilitate—faith cannot be correctly understood apart from a kind of knowledge that properly and logically precedes it: it "is precisely for the sake of faith that the importance of rational knowledge of its basis has to be emphasized."[18] It is because faith is based upon genuine knowledge of a definable content, which is objectively the case regardless of whether or not it is ever known, that we are justified in speaking of the assurance of faith at all. Closely related to this point is Pannenberg's contention that the Lutheran *pro me* was never intended to be apotheosized in isolation from the *extra me* of faith.[19] From Pannenberg's standpoint, his corrective of existentialist excess follows naturally once we appreciate that the "logic of faith and its psychology must be distinguished."[20]

Pannenberg's stance thereby provides the basis for a position concerning faith's relation to historical knowledge that is the exact opposite of the view shared by Lessing and Kierkegaard. Christian faith must be based upon adequate historical knowledge of the past to which it refers. In contrast to Lessing, Pannenberg is saying that faith is dependent for both its truth and its meaning upon reference to the past; as opposed to both Lessing and Kierkegaard, he maintains that faith is dependent as well upon empirical inquiry into the past. He is arguing that to require reference to the past without also assuming theological responsibility for inquiry into the past is potentially to undermine the need to have the historical reference. "The reference of the Christian faith to history unavoidably carries with it the demand that the believer must not try to save himself from historical-critical questions by means of some 'invulnerable area'—otherwise it will lose its historical basis."[21]

Pannenberg further maintains that the theologian does not gain access to the relevant past through a privileged, "pneumatic" historiography, or through the kind of special pleading that produces historical claims on the basis of theological needs. He more than once cites the criticism of Martin Kähler offered by Wilhelm Herrmann, who suggests that Kähler's position may tempt us "to base our faith on something that is perhaps not a historical fact at all, but is itself a product of faith."[22] Faith, claims Pannenberg, cannot legitimately "ascertain anything about events of the past that would perhaps be inaccessible to the historian."[23] Instead, faith has its basis "in an event which is a matter for knowing and which becomes known to us only by more or less adequate information," arrived at through secular inquiry.[24] This viewpoint reflects Pannenberg's admission that he "cannot understand any knowledge as other than 'natural,' "[25] which, in turn, reflects his conviction that the truth is one.[26] In short, he has no room in his theological program for such a notion as "the eyes of faith."

Pannenberg's position thus implies that Christian faith could, in principle, be empirically falsified. This is for him an altogether acceptable result, since it is the necessary price we pay if we are really to be asserting anything in the confession of faith. Without the possibility that the believer might be wrong, there is literally nothing to be gained from being right.[27] For Pannenberg, the empirical irrefutability of faith, fashionable in modern Protestant thought and clearly present in the work of both Lessing and Kierkegaard, can be purchased only at the cost of rendering faith entirely in terms of moral or existential interiority. This move to the interior, however, entails invoking what for Pannenberg is the utterly repugnant principle that faith has no basis "outside" itself, but serves as its own ground or basis. Retreat to an inner, private, hidden dimension of the religious self effectively waters faith down into mere "existential resolve," producing "the ruinous consequence that faith grounds itself, and so distorts that which is essential to it, viz., its dependence upon a truth outside itself." In other words, the strategies that Lessing, Kierkegaard, and such successors of theirs as Herrmann and Bultmann adopt to neutralize historical-critical difficulties are a greater threat to faith than historical criticism itself.

What we have here is a correlation between, first, the view that faith must be based on prior knowledge, the acquisition of which does not depend upon our already having the "eyes of faith," and, second, a repudiation of an inflated subject of faith and of attendant appeals to hidden, private recesses within the religious believer.

Put differently, Pannenberg is attempting to reorient us toward the "outer" history that was displaced by the attention devoted to the "inner," personal history in the traditions of Lessing and Kierkegaard. To be interested in knowledge of historical events as the true basis of faith is simultaneously to suspect whatever is private, hidden, and individualistic.

The themes and categories elicited by the present study help to illuminate the even deeper divisions separating Pannenberg from the traditions of Lessing and Kierkegaard. His turn toward the outer world of public history, his insistence that faith is properly grounded in knowledge, and his suspicion of appeals to human interiority all suggest the anti-Kantian and, finally, the anti-Cartesian character of his thinking. On the theological side, Pannenberg's major emphases constitute a repudiation of the latent yet powerful role played by pietistic traditions within the development of modern

Protestant theology. Not only Lessing and Kant, but the enormously influential figure of Schleiermacher, are sophisticated products of the pietist appeal to inner, heart-felt religion.[28] And, from Pannenberg's perspective at least, even Bultmann might be considered a kind of neo-pietist in Heideggerian disguise. The Cartesian-Kantian-existentialist element on the philosophical side, and the pietistic element, buttressed by a distorted Luther, on the theological side, merge in a way that undermines dogmatic thinking and turns theology into nothing more than a sophisticated form of introspection.[29]

With specific regard to historical-critical difficulties, this subjectivist tradition in theology has been aided enormously by Kantian epistemology. Accordingly, Pannenberg attacks the distinctions between "being and value" and between "historical fact and historical meaning" which have been sustained by this dualistic epistemology and, in turn, have fortified the distinction between the eyes of faith and secular historiography.[30] An exaggerated emphasis on historical meanings at the expense of a responsible concern for the original facts—exemplified, thinks Pannenberg, by the uses and abuses to which Kähler's distinction between *Historie* and *Geschichte* has been subject[31]—dovetails dangerously with the appeal to the private, inner self in the accounting of faith. The result is to undermine interest in any aspect of faith that is not self-reflexive, which, for Pannenberg, is to abandon interest in the sole legitimate basis of faith.

In basing Christian faith upon historical knowledge, Pannenberg would appear to be threatened by the temporal ditch, separating the present-day believer from religiously momentous events of the past. In other words, precisely because of his differences with both Lessing and Kierkegaard, Pannenberg appears subject to a difficulty to which they were effectively immune—namely, the hazards of historical reconstruction and the adjudication of matters of fact.

To a certain extent, this is true and is part of the cognitive risk Pannenberg is happy to accept as the price to pay for a confession of faith that really confesses something. Pannenberg is remarkably optimistic about what we can actually establish about the past through historical means, claiming even to have a historical proof for the resurrection of Jesus.[32] Reflecting the intellectual openness of the liberal tradition in modern Protestantism, Pannenberg agrees that the "believer cannot want to prohibit any historical question, no matter how it be fashioned."[33] But in a stunning contrast to the normal way in which this intellectual openness is made theologically tolerable—which is to invoke an epistemological dualism that insulates faith from historical-critical results—Pannenberg goes on to claim that

> the believer can only trust that the facticity of the event on which he bases himself will continually be upheld throughout the progress of historical research. The history of critical-historical investigation of the biblical witnesses, especially of the New Testament, by no means gives the appearance of discouraging such confidence.[34]

Clearly, Pannenberg's views concerning the theological rewards of New Testament research are as idiosyncratic as his views concerning faith's relation to historical knowledge.

Here we come up against the most substantive theological alteration effected by Pannenberg. This concerns the problem of revelation. As the cases of Lessing and, especially, Kierkegaard have indicated, the ultimate reason that historical research is for them theologically blind is that not even an eyewitness to a historical revelation could, by virtue of chronological immediacy, "see" God in Jesus. Even less, then, could historical reconstruction detect revelation. There is, in the influential Kierkegaardian version of the relation between history and revelation, the metaphysical impasse between time and eternity, prohibiting even the most successful historian from catching the slightest glimpse of the divine.

Consequently, when Pannenberg endorses the positive correlation between theology and historical research, he appears to be saying that the historian qua historian can detect the divine presence or activity. He appears, in other words, to be bridging the metaphysical incommensurability between time and eternity, or between humanity and God, that informs not merely Kierkegaard's viewpoint but the more recent Bultmannian principle that God acts within history but never appears from the standpoint of historical research.

Pannenberg is indeed claiming that the secular historian can, in fact, detect revelation. However, this claim is not based on the defeat of the metaphysical dualism in terms of which Kierkegaard and his successors pose the relation between history and revelation. For this dualism, aided as it is by Kant's phenomena-noumena dichotomy, shapes the issue in a manner that Pannenberg repudiates: dualism with respect to history and revelation is no more acceptable to him than are the dualisms that effect the divorce between historical fact and historical meaning, or that generate the inflation of the inner subject of faith over against outer, public history.[35] A "splitting up of historical consciousness into a detection of facts and an

evaluation of them is intolerable," says Pannenberg, not only because this leads to "merely subjective interpretation," but also because it "is based on the futile aim of the positivist historians to
ascertain bare facts without meaning in history."[36]

In other words, Pannenberg does not overcome the problem of
history and revelation by solving someone else's Kantian difficulty.
Instead, he proposes a new view of revelation that prohibits the
dualistic difficulty from arising in the first place. The point is not
that he has overcome the dualisms that structure contemporary discussions of Lessing's ditch; instead, the key issue is that he proposes
a view of revelation, together with a unified theory of truth, that
prevent those dualisms from dictating how we reflect on history and
revelation. Putting God back into history—subsequent to disentan-
gling God from the snares of human subjectivity—is accompanied
by putting God back into historiography as well.

Accordingly, revelation for Pannenberg is not a divine addendum
to history, a hidden, noumenal moment *within* history, or a private,
experiential or existential moment *inside* the self. Such formulations
as these are either hopelessly subjective or else perpetuate the mistaken notion that revelation is something other than, or in addition
to, history. For Pannenberg, all of history *as such* is revelation, in
the sense that universal history is simultaneously God's self-
disclosure.[37] This understanding of universal history as itself revelation—which places Pannenberg in an acknowledged and self-con-
scious indebtedness to Hegel[38]—coordinates with his rejection of a
bifurcation between historical event and historical meaning. The
determining factor in grasping revelation is not a dichotomy between event and meaning, or *Historie* and *Geschichte*, but an appre-
ciation of history as a whole, which prohibits isolating individual
historical events outside the context of universal history.[39] The key
term here is *context*: understanding the identity of events and their
significance depends upon appreciating the traditions within which
historical events occur and are understood.[40] It is primarily for this
reason that Pannenberg refuses to understand the life of Jesus except in the context of the history of Israel, which, in turn, leads to
the kind of rapprochement between Christian theology and Old Testament studies that has been impossible in recent decades within a
Bultmannian setting.

Pannenberg's emphasis on universal history as itself the locus of
revelation necessarily requires theological interest in the "end" of
history. This result is demanded by the contextualism of Pannenberg's position, with its emphasis on the history of traditions and

the interconnectedness of all historical events.[41] Pannenberg's contextualism is not intended to underwrite simply the epistemological claim that we do not truly *know* the meaning of an event until the end of history, for this would be to reintroduce the division between an event and its significance. His contextualism is primarily intended to underwrite the ontological claim that no historical event truly *is* what it is until the end of history.[42] An obvious implication of this, characteristic of Pannenberg's position from the earliest stages of his career, is that revelation itself fully occurs only at the end of history.[43] Jesus' resurrection is the "proleptic appearance" of this end of history, and therefore is the key event referred to by Christian faith.[44] In light of Pannenberg's attitude toward the relation between faith and knowledge, the connection between the resurrection of Jesus and the culmination of universal history suggests the very important and perhaps decisive role played by his historical proof for the resurrection within his theology as a whole. That so much should turn on something so open to serious question from the surrounding culture reveals, for better or worse, the extent to which Pannenberg wants to make Christian theology a genuine partner in the culture's general quest for knowledge.

This is not the place to track down and analyze the obvious—and not so obvious—questions and difficulties raised by Pannenberg's views on faith, history, and revelation. As with my accounts of Troeltsch's principles of historical research and of Ogden's christology, my summary here of Pannenberg's position has been designed primarily to lift the several issues associated with Lessing's ditch into a more contemporary setting. Pannenberg's standpoint, whatever its flaws, is provocative precisely because it boldly repudiates the theological fashions introduced by Lessing and Kierkegaard. Moreover, as the different features of Pannenberg's position fall into place, we can more readily appreciate the interlocking character of the several elements implicit in any reaction to Lessing's ditches and their associated problems. Pannenberg's viewpoint is perhaps particularly instructive in the way it suggests the continuing predominance of the motifs of "inner" and "outer" in the accounting of faith's relation to historical events and historical knowledge. He expressly correlates an appeal to outer or public historical events, and knowledge about them, with a rejection of theological appeals to inner or subjective states in the rendering of faith. In contrast, both Lessing and Kierkegaard expressly turn to inner, hidden states of personal consciousness in their retreat from theological reliance on knowledge of outer historical events.

Even in Pannenberg's case, however, we have seen one of the fundamental morals of this study illustrated once again. He arrives at a position on historical knowledge *subsequent* to establishing an angle of vision on, first, the issue of historical revelation and, second, the question of the relationship between Christianity's truth claims and natural human modes of insight or wisdom. His position on the issue of historical knowledge is a function of his stand on these other matters. In this, he is at one with Lessing and Kierkegaard, as well as with Bultmann and Ogden.

CONCLUDING REMARKS

Lessing and his successors represent stages in the evolution of a problem, moments in the dialectical development of a theme intrinsic to Christian theology. Although the judgment that Christianity is a historical religion is correct in any age, the force and point of this judgment are highly variable, depending upon historical context. Complex developments in the century preceding Lessing insured that, by his time, even a reasonably well-informed account of Christianity's relationship to history—let alone Lessing's nuanced and perhaps intentionally ambiguous account—would open up an array of problem areas, not just one. This is why the legacy of his image of the ugly ditch is a confusing one. Kierkegaard's arrival on the scene would guarantee a unique variation on the theme of faith and history, a product not only of his Hegelian time and place but of his extraordinary individual genius as well. In his depiction of the problem, as well as in his fashioning of a solution, Kierkegaard would explore terrain untouched even by Lessing. In retrospect, it is likewise clear that Kierkegaard's arrival would ultimately provide a disproportionate measure of the fresh guidance and inspiration sought out by a postwar theological community, hungry for new insight and open to the language of paradox and offense. Theology since 1918 has, in large measure, been an ongoing debate over what to do about paradox.

A truly definitive account of these issues would pursue in far greater detail the specific historical circumstances of which Lessing and Kierkegaard were each a product and to which each was responding. I have been content simply to separate out the various strands constituting their often confusing or misleading discussions of faith and history, and to indicate in brief compass the relevance of this sorting process for twentieth-century theology. Such an ap-

proach can clarify but not explain: it can clarify a body of conceptual material, but it cannot possibly explain why some issues connected with the topic are more evident and pressing at some times
than at others. Presumably, only historical understanding can do
that job. Still, the current inquiry certainly shares with a genuinely
historical approach the capacity to highlight, not only the ambiguity of Lessing's own image, but the very different things that
"ditch" imagery can convey, depending upon the theological requirements of the moment. Thus, Lessing's image of the ditch
should hardly be relied upon as a handy code for signaling "a problem." It should instead be treated as an invitation to greater speci-
ficity. For shifts in theological fashions are not simply a function of
new solutions to fixed problems, but of fresh statements of these
problems as well. Ditch imagery itself changes from setting to setting, both reflecting and keeping in motion the dialectic of Christianity's relation to history.

If it is the fate of Christian faith to be tied to history, it does not
necessarily follow that it is the fate of theology to be tied to ditch
imagery. The weak form of the ultimate conclusion of this study
recapitulates the point just made: ditch imagery does not stand for
a certain "lasting issue" to which different thinkers have different
responses; rather, it is itself subject to change and alteration, depending upon the operative theological needs and aims. The stronger form of the conclusion is that we have passed through the heyday
of ditch imagery, and ought to leave both the heyday and the image
behind us: ditch imagery itself, on this view, is part of the problem,
and not a handy description of some other problem. In this case, as I
indicated at the very outset of this study, we should not be in the
business of seeking technical solutions to "the problem" of faith and
history, any more than we should be bogged down in methodological dismay over the presuppositions of historical research. We
should instead be busy at the task of dismantling the conceptual
framework that keeps the proper questions about history and revelation from ever coming into view. And the first step in this direction is probably something more like irony than technical virtuos-
ity. Whether or not a theology located primarily in the Academy is
up to this more radical task is difficult to say.

Notes

CHAPTER 1

1. Lessing, "Über den Beweis des Geistes und der Kraft," in *Gesammelte Werke*, vol. 8, ed. Paul Rilla (Berlin: Aufbau-Verlag, 1956), pp. 12, 14. English translation, "On the Proof of the Spirit and of Power," in *Lessing's Theological Writings*, ed. and trans. Henry Chadwick (Stanford: Stanford University Press, 1956), pp. 53, 55. Hereafter cited as "Proof," with page number in both Rilla and Chadwick following.

2. See Kierkegaard's reference to Lessing's (supposed) final words in *Concluding Unscientific Postscript*, trans. David W. Swenson and Walter Lowrie (Princeton: Princeton University Press, 1968), p. 94.

3. Van A. Harvey, *The Historian and the Believer* (New York: Macmillan, 1966), p. 17.

4. Quoted by Henry Chadwick in his "Introduction" to *Lessing's Theological Writings*, p. 32. Coleridge's remark is inscribed in the margin of his copy of Lessing's essay.

5. Hans W. Frei, *The Eclipse of Biblical Narrative* (New Haven: Yale University Press, 1974), p. 116.

6. Kierkegaard, *Postscript*, p. 26n.

7. Wilhelm Herrmann, *The Communion of the Christian with God*, ed. Robert T. Voelkel (Philadelphia: Fortress Press, 1971), p. 72.

8. For a helpful clarification of Herrmann on this and other points, see Daniel L. Deegan, "Wilhelm Herrmann: A Reassessment," *Scottish Journal of Theology* 19 (1966): 188–203. For a discussion of Herrmann's location on the spectrum from Luther to Bultmann, see A.O. Dyson, *The Immortality of the Past* (London: SCM Press, LTD, 1974), pp. 62ff.

9. Martin Kähler, *The So-Called Historical Jesus and the Historic Biblical Christ*, ed. and trans. Carl E. Braaten (Philadelphia: Fortress Press, 1964).

10. For a helpful summary of this and related points, see Leander E. Keck's "Editor's Introduction" to his translation of David Friedrich Strauss, *The Christ of Faith and the Jesus of History* (Philadelphia: Fortress Press, 1977), pp. xv–cvi, esp. lxxxii–cvi. See also Daniel L. Deegan, "Martin Kähler: Kerygma and Gospel History," *Scottish Journal of Theology* 16 (1963): 50–67.

11. Bultmann would maintain that he endeavored throughout his career to "carry further the tradition of historical-critical research as it was practiced by the 'liberal' theology and to make our more recent theological knowledge fruitful for it." See his "Autobiographical Reflections," in *Existence and Faith*, ed. and trans. Schubert M. Ogden (Cleveland: World, 1960), p. 288.

12. Bultmann, "Liberal Theology and the Latest Theological Movement," *Faith and Understanding*, trans. Louise Pettibone Smith (New York; Harper and Row, 1969), p. 30; emphasis Bultmann's.

13. Bultmann, "The Primitive Christian Kerygma and the Historical Jesus," in *The Historical Jesus and the Kerygmatic Christ*, ed. Carl E. Braaten and Roy Harrisville (Nashville: Abingdon Press, 1964), p. 25.

14. The most useful single reference for grasping Pannenberg's general position on this point remains "Hermeneutic and Universal History," in *Basic Questions in Theology*, vol. 1, trans. George H. Kehm (Philadelphia: Fortress Press, 1970), pp. 96–136. See also "On Historical and Theological Hermeneutic," in *Basic Questions*, vol. 1, pp. 137–81; and "Insight and Faith," in *Basic Questions*, vol. 2 (1971), pp. 28–45. I discuss Pannenberg's position in greater detail in chapter 7.

15. Harvey, *The Historian and the Believer*, p. 17.

16. James M. Robinson, *Kerygma und Historischer Jesus*, 2d ed. (Zürich: Zwingli Verlag, 1967). From quite a different vantage point, other biblical scholars (such as Brevard Childs, James D. Smart, Walter Wink, and Peter Stuhlmacher) have for some time now been bemoaning the absence of any theological dividends from the historical-critical approach to scripture.

17. Robinson, *A New Quest of the Historical Jesus* (London: SCM Press, LTD, 1959), p. 92.

18. Robinson, "The Recent Debate on the 'New Quest,'" *Journal of Bible and Religion* 30 (1962): 202.

19. Ibid., p. 206.

20. Robinson, *Kerygma und Historischer Jesus*, 2d ed., pp. 53–54.

21. *Webster's Seventh New Collegiate Dictionary* (Springfield: G. and C. Merriam, 1965).

22. "Proof," pp. 10, 51.

23. Lessing originally wrote the essay in response to a pamphlet written in 1777 by Johann David Schumann, director of the Hanover Lyceum, entitled "On the Evidence of the Proofs for the Truth of the Christian Religion." Drawing on traditional orthodox conceptions of historical proofs for the truth of Christianity, Schumann endeavored to rebut the attack on Christianity surfacing at that time in the "Fragments" of Hermann Samuel Reimarus that Lessing was publishing. See Henry Allison, *Lessing and the Enlightenment* (Ann Arbor: University of Michigan Press, 1966), p. 101.

24. Frei, *The Eclipse of Biblical Narrative*, pp. 57–58.

25. This is immediately evident on the title page of Kierkegaard's *Philosophical Fragments*, trans. David W. Swenson and Howard Hong (Princeton: Princeton University Press, 1962).

26. For example, Richard Campbell, "Lessing's Problem and Kierkegaard's Answer," *Scottish Journal of Theology* 19 (1966): 35–54, esp. 44–48; Peter C. Hodgson, *The Formation of Historical Theology* (New York; Harper and Row, 1966), p. 271; Klaus Penzel, "Church History in Context: The Case of Philip Schaff," in *Our Common Heritage as Christians: Essays in Honor of Albert C. Outler*, ed. John Deschner, Leroy T. Howe, and Klaus Penzel (New York: Oxford University Press, 1975), p. 243. A much more nuanced treatment is offered by David Pailin, "Lessing's Ditch Revisited: The Problem of Faith and History," in *Theology and Change: Essays in Memory of Alan Richardson*, ed. R.H. Preston (London: SCM Press, LTD, 1975), pp. 78–103. See my own initial discussion of the ditch, from which the current study has developed, "Lessing, Kierkegaard, and the 'Ugly Ditch': A Reexamination," *Journal of Religion* 59 (1979): 324–34.

27. See the concluding chapter of Schweitzer's classic, *Quest of the Historical Jesus* (New York: Macmillan, 1956).

28. Frei, *The Eclipse of Biblical Narrative*, chs. 3 and 8; Allison, *Lessing and the Enlightenment*, ch. 1.

29. "Proof," pp. 12, 15; pp. 53, 55.

30. Lessing, *Nathan der Weise*, ed. Peter Demetz (Frankfurt/M and Berlin: Verlag Ullstein, 1966). I pursue the issue of "inner truth" in considerably more detail in chapters 2 and 3.

31. A capsule statement of Lessing's attitude toward neology is a comment in a letter to his brother, Karl: "With orthodoxy, thank God, things were fairly well settled. A curtain had been drawn between it and philosophy, behind which each could go his own way without disturbing the other. But what is happening now? They are tearing down this curtain, and under the pretext of making us rational Christians, they are making us very irrational philosophers." Cited and translated by Allison, *Lessing and the Enlightenment*, p. 84.

32. For example, Bultmann, "New Testament and Mythology," *Kerygma and Myth*, ed. Hans Werner Bartsch and trans. Reginald H. Fuller (New York: Harper and Row, 1961), pp. 33–44.

33. See Bultmann's response to Kamlah in *Kerygma and Myth*, pp. 25ff. Bultmann is responding to Kamlah's *Christentum und Selbstbehauptung* (Frankfurt: Verlag Klostermann, 1940). For a discussion of the relation between Bultmann and Kamlah, see Schubert M. Ogden, *Christ Without Myth* (New York: Harper and Row, 1961), pp. 70ff.

34. As I attempt to show in chapter 6, the real issue here is neither the nature of faith nor the lengths to which demythologization is to be taken, but the concept of revelation.

35. A good example of this approach is Schubert M. Ogden's *The Reality of God* (New York: Harper and Row, 1966), especially the lead essay. Roman Catholic versions of the same general approach include David Tracy's *Blessed Rage for Order* (New York: Seabury, 1975) and *The Analogical Imagination* (New York: Crossroads, 1981) as well as Karl Rahner's *Foundations of the Christian Faith: An Introduction to the Idea of Christianity*, trans. W.V. Dych (New York: Seabury, 1978).

36. The oddity involved in the way liberal theologians give up the distinctiveness of Christianity, in the pursuit of intelligible contact with the surrounding culture, is neatly pinpointed by Alasdair MacIntyre in "The Fate of Theism," in MacIntyre and Paul Ricoeur, *The Religious Significance of Atheism* (New York and London: Columbia University Press, 1969), pp. 3–29. See also MacIntyre's earlier essay, "God and the Theologians," reprinted in MacIntyre, *Against the Self-Images of the Age* (Notre Dame: University of Notre Dame Press, 1978), pp. 12–26. A more detailed approach to these matters, along similar interpretive lines, is offered in part 2 of Jeffrey Stout's *The Flight from Authority* (Notre Dame: University of Notre Dame Press, 1981).

37. The example is MacIntyre's.

38. Richard Rorty, "Keeping Philosophy Pure," *Yale Review* 65 (1976): 347.

39. Van A. Harvey, "The Alienated Theologian," in *The Future of Philosophical Theology*, ed. Robert A. Evans (Philadelphia: Westminster Press, 1971), pp. 113–43.

CHAPTER 2

1. Lessing, "Proof," pp. 10, 51.

2. Ibid., pp. 10, 51–52.

3. Ibid., pp. 11, 52.

4. Ibid., pp. 11–12, 53.

5. See Richard Swinburne's discussion of four kinds of historical evidence and their relation to religious claims, in *The Concept of Miracle* (London: Macmillan, 1970), pp. 33ff.

6. "Proof," pp. 11, 52.

7. Ibid.

8. See Hume, book 10, *Inquiry Concerning Human Understanding* (New York: Bobbs-Merrill, 1955).

9. Hans Frei, *The Eclipse of Biblical Narrative* (New Haven: Yale University Press, 1974), pp. 52–53.

10. "Proof," pp. 14, 54.

11. Ibid.

12. Ibid., pp. 12, 53.

13. On Lessing's debt to Spinoza and Leibniz, see Henry Allison, *Lessing and the Enlightenment* (Ann Arbor: University of Michigan Press, 1966), pp. 67–78, 123–35; and A. Schilson, *Geschichte im Horizont der Vorsehung: G.E. Lessings Beitrag zu einer Theologie der Geschichte* (Mainz: Matthias-Grünewald Verlag, 1974), pp. 215–19.

14. "Proof," pp. 12, 53.

15. Ibid., pp. 12, 55.

16. In the present context, a "metaphysical" problem—over against what I have been calling temporal and epistemological problems—cannot be resolved through factual inquiry, since it concerns the clash or impasse between different orders of truth (for example, historical truth and religious truth) and, thus, the problem of determining an all-embracing view of reality that might resolve such an impasse from a higher standpoint. A metaphysical problem, in short, requires a metaphysical and not an empirical solution.

17. "Proof," pp. 12, 53.

18. Ibid.

19. Allison, *Lessing and the Enlightenment*, p. 121, speaks of Lessing's "rejection of the traditional concept of revelation" as "a logical consequence of Lessing's monistic metaphysics, which antedated but was profoundly enriched by his study of Spinoza." An alternative interpretation, which allows for a genuinely transcendent God within Lessing's viewpoint, is offered by Helmut Thielicke, *Offenbarung, Vernunft, und Existenz: Studien zur Religionsphilosophie Lessings*, 4th ed. (Gütersloh: Carl Bertelsmann Verlag, 1957). There are summaries of recent Lessing interpretation in Schilson, *Geschichte im Horizont der Vorsehung*, pp. 21–35, and in Leonard P. Wessel, *G.E. Lessing's Theology: A Reinterpretation* (The Hague and Paris: Mouton, 1977), pp. 13ff.

20. Lessing, "Die Erziehung des Menschengeschlechts," *Gesammelte Werke*, vol. 8, ed. Paul Rilla (Berlin: Aufbau-Verlag, 1956), p. 592; English translation, "The Education of the Human Race," *Lessing's Theological Writings*, ed. and trans. Henry Chadwick (Stanford: Stanford University Press, 1956), p. 83.

21. At a later point in "The Education of the Human Race," Lessing refers to religious truths "which human reason would never have reached on its own" (*Gesammelte Werke*, vol. 8, pp. 610–11; English translation, *Lessing's Theological Writings*, p. 95); this is an apparent contradiction of his earlier point that has been interpreted in a variety of ways. See, for example, Allison, *Lessing and the Enlightenment*, pp. 147ff.; Chadwick, "Editor's Introduction," *Lessing's Theological Writings*, pp. 39ff.; and Thielicke, *Offenbarung, Vernunft, und Existenz*, pp. 33ff.

22. Allison, *Lessing and the Enlightenment*, pp. 121–22.

23. This comment appears in Lessing's "Gegensätze des Herausgebers" in his edition of the "Fragments" of Hermann Samuel Reimarus, taken from Reimarus's *Apologie oder Schutzschrift für die Vernünftigen Verehrer Gottes.* Lessing, *Gesammelte Werke*, vol. 7, p. 813. English translation taken from Allison, *Lessing and the Enlightenment*, p. 96.

24. Lessing, "Die Erziehung des Menschengeschlechts," pp. 597, 603–5; English translation, "The Education of the Human Race," pp. 87, 91.

25. See Michel Despland, *Kant on History and Religion* (Montreal and London: McGill-Queen's University Press, 1973), esp. chs. 8–10; and G.E. Michalson, Jr., *The Historical Dimensions of a Rational Faith: The Role of History in Kant's Religious Thought* (Washington, D.C.: University Press of America, 1977), chs. 2–3.

26. Kenneth L. Schmitz, "The Conceptualization of Religious Mystery: An Essay on Hegel's Philosophy of Religion," in *The Legacy of Hegel*, ed. J.J. O'Malley, K.W. Algozin, H.P. Kainz, and L.C. Rice (The Hague: Martinus Nijhoff, 1973), pp. 108–36; John E. Smith, "Hegel's Critique of Kant," *Review of Metaphysics* 26 (1973): 438–60.

27. Stephen Crites, "The Gospel According to Hegel," *Journal of Religion* 46 (1966): 246–63; Crites, *In the Twilight of Christendom: Hegel vs. Kierkegaard on Faith and History* (Chambersburg: American Academy of Religion, 1971).

28. Michalson, *The Historical Dimensions of a Rational Faith*, ch. 4.

29. "The designation *positive* is given appropriately to those religions which in claiming to be based on a special divine disclosure are made dependent on the contingencies of history." Bernard M.G. Reardon, *Hegel's Philosophy of Religion* (New York: Barnes and Noble, 1977), p. 106. See also the discussions in Frei, *The Eclipse of Biblical Narrative*, pp. 57–59; and Garrett Green, "Editor's Introduction" to J.G. Fichte, *Attempt at a Critique of All Revelation*, trans. Green (Cambridge: Cambridge University Press, 1977), pp. 28–29. In large part, the problem of positivity was what Kant was addressing in his *Religion within the Limits of Reason Alone* and what Hegel was grappling with throughout the series of youthful essays commonly known as the "early theological writings"—and, perhaps, throughout his entire authorship.

30. For further discussion of this point, see Friedrich Traub, "Geschichtswahrheiten und Vernunftswahrheiten bei Lessing," *Zeitschrift für Theologie und Kirche* 28 (1920): 193–207; and Wessel, *G.E. Lessing's Theology: A Reinterpretation*, pp. 120ff.

31. "Proof," pp. 15–16, 55–56. For further discussion of this mathematical analogy, see chapter 3.

32. Again, Thielicke, *Offenbarung, Vernunft, und Existenz*, offers an alternative to this basically rationalist interpretation of Lessing.

CHAPTER 3

1. Lessing, "Proof," pp. 13, 54.

2. Ibid., pp. 14, 54.

3. Ibid., pp. 14, 54–55.

4. "Proof," pp. 14, 55.

5. See Karl Barth's discussion of Lessing's distinction between "the religion of Christ" and "the Christian religion," in *Protestant Thought: From Rousseau to Ritschl*, trans. Brian Cozens (New York: Simon and Schuster, 1959), p. 125.

6. Lessing's employment of a dramatic form for the expression of religious ideas came in the wake of an order from the censor's office at Brunswick to cease exchang-

ing public polemics with Pastor Johann Goeze of Hamburg. The exchange had been instigated by Goeze's efforts to defend Christian orthodoxy against the views coming to expression in the "Fragments" of Hermann Samuel Reimarus, published by Lessing. See Barth, *Protestant Thought: From Rousseau to Ritschl*, p. 122; and Henry Allison, *Lessing and the Enlightenment* (Ann Arbor: University of Michigan Press, 1966), pp. 107ff.

7. It should be kept in mind, however, that—following the intervention of the censor's office—Lessing had little choice but to cast his religious ideas in dramatic form.

8. Lessing's pioneering work in aesthetics, *Laokoon, oder Über die Grenzen der Malerei und Poesie*, had been published a full decade prior to the appearance of "On the Proof of the Spirit and of Power."

9. "Die Erziehung des Menschengeschlechts," *Gesammelte Werke*, vol. 8, ed. Paul Rilla (Berlin: Aufbau-Verlag, 1956), pp. 590–615; English trans., "The Education of the Human Race," *Lessing's Theological Writings*, ed. and trans. Henry Chadwick (Stanford: Stanford University Press, 1956). pp. 82–98.

10. Allison, *Lessing and the Enlightenment*, pp. 130–35, argues persuasively that, far from being ad hoc or confused, Lessing's religious thought is the result of his adaptation of Leibnizian perspectivalism.

11. For example, Van A. Harvey, *The Historian and the Believer* (New York: Macmillan, 1966).

12. Lessing, *Nathan der Weise*, ed. Peter Demetz (Frankfurt/M and Berlin: Verlag Ullstein, 1966).

13. The centerpiece of *Nathan der Weise* is Boccaccio's "parable of the rings," adapted by Lessing in a way that suggests that the truth of a religion is determined by the sincerity and conduct of its adherents and not by the literal accuracy of its doctrinal claims. The true or genuine ring, Lessing has Nathan say,

"...hatte die geheime Kraft, vor Gott
Und Menschen angenehm zu machen, *wer*
In dieser Zuversicht ihn trug."
Nathan der Weise, p. 64; emphasis added.

14. The Leibnizian interpretation of Lessing offered by Allison, *Lessing and the Enlightenment*, pp. 130ff., further buttresses this point.

15. "Proof," pp. 15–16, 55–56.

16. Ibid., pp. 15, 55.

17. Ibid.

18. Lessing, "Gegensätze des Herausgebers" (Lessing's introduction to the "Fragments" of Reimarus), *Gesammelte Werke*, vol. 7, p. 813. English translation taken from Allison, *Lessing and the Enlightenment*, p. 95.

19. Translation from Allison, *Lessing and the Enlightenment*, p. 96.

20. "Self-authenticating" here is an Enlightenment parallel to Protestant orthodoxy's appeal to "illumination," produced by a Bible understood to be its "own testimony." See Paul Helm, *The Varieties of Belief* (London: George Allen and Unwin, LTD, 1973), ch. 6. As Helm points out (p. 105), much depends upon whether a claim for self-authentication is being made for an experience or for a proposition.

21. Lessing, "Das Testament Johannis," *Gesammelte Werke*, vol. 8, pp. 17–23; English translation, "The Testament of John," *Lessing's Theological Writings*, pp. 57–61.

22. I. Kant, "What is Enlightenment?" in *Kant on History*, ed. and trans. Lewis White Beck (New York: Bobbs-Merrill, 1963), p. 3.

23. Lessing, "Gegensätze des Herausgebers," p. 813.

24. I say·"in an odd sort of way" since Hegel would view the moral will from the substantially altered standpoint effected by his displacement of Kantian *Moralität* with the more historically oriented *Sittlichkeit*.

25. Georg Lukács, *The Young Hegel: Studies in the Relations between Dialectics and Economics*, trans. Rodney Livingstone (Cambridge: MIT Press, 1976), p. 18.

26. Concerning the varieties of reductionism in religious matters, see Helm, *The Varieties of Belief*, p. 43; and J.C. Thornton, "Religious Belief and 'Reductionism,' " *Sophia* 5 (1966): 3–16. Thornton (p. 9) says that "there is certainly something to be said for regarding as 'reductionist' any analysis of Christian belief which claims that the truth of Christianity is logically independent of the truth of all historical beliefs."

27. Kant *Critique of Pure Reason*, trans. Norman Kemp-Smith (New York: St. Martin's Press, 1965), A829-B857, p. 650.

28. Depending upon one's theological loyalties, this Kantian tradition could be said to have reached a reductio ad absurdum in the existentialist theology of Fritz Buri. See the exposition and evaluation of Buri, with particular reference to the objectivity problem, in Charley D. Hardwick, *Faith and Objectivity: Fritz Buri and the Hermeneutical Foundations of a Radical Theology* (The Hague: Martinus Nijhoff, 1972).

29. Helmut Thielicke, *The Evangelical Faith*, vol. 1, ed. and trans. Geoffrey Bromiley (Grand Rapids: William B. Eerdmans, 1974), part 1.

30. Concerning the "regulative" character of religious belief, see Helm, *The Varieties of Belief*, p. 42.

31. Thielicke, *The Evangelical Faith*, ch. 3, esp. pp. 44–45.

32. Ernest Gellner, *The Devil in Modern Philosophy*, ed. I.C. Jarvie and Joseph Agassi (London: Routledge and Kegan Paul, 1974), p. 40.

33. Thielicke, *The Evangelical Faith*, pp. 42–43.

34. The "left" includes not only left-wing Bultmannians, who *want* to push Bultmann in this direction (for example, Fritz Buri), but a very different sort of critic, such as the "later" Alasdair MacIntyre, who spots the fact that theologians like Bultmann have successfully purchased the "logical invulnerability" of Christianity, but only at the cost of "emptiness." See MacIntyre, "Is Understanding Religion Compatible with Believing?" in *Rationality*, ed. Bryan R. Wilson (New York: Harper and Row, 1971)), pp. 62–77, esp. pp. 74–75.

35. For example, Karl Barth, "Rudolph Bultmann—An Attempt to Understand Him," in *Kerygma and Myth*, vol. 2, ed. Hans Werner Bartsch, and trans. Reginald H. Fuller (London: SPCK, 1962), pp. 83–132.

36. Van A. Harvey, "The Pathos of Liberal Theology," *Journal of Religion* 56 (1976): 382–91.

37. Various themes bearing on this dilemma have been woven together in the illuminating study by Jeffrey Stout, *The Flight from Authority* (Notre Dame: University of Notre Dame Press, 1981).

CHAPTER 4

1. Kierkegaard, *Philosophical Fragments*, trans. David Swenson and Howard Hong (Princeton: Princeton University Press, 1962). Hereafter referred to as *PF*. Since my major aim here is to chart the structure of a certain response to the ditch and associated problems, and not to undertake a major piece of "Kierkegaard interpreta-

tion" based on original sources, I shall simply be bracketing the well-known difficulties associated with Kierkegaard's pseudonyms and his theory of indirect communication. Like Lessing's "On the Proof of the Spirit and of Power," Kierkegaard's two chief Johannes Climacus works—the *Fragments* and the *Concluding Unscientific Postscript*—will be explored for their own sake.

2. Kierkegaard, *Concluding Unscientific Postscript*, trans. David Swenson and Walter Lowrie (Princeton: Princeton University Press, 1968), pp. 18–20. Hereafter referred to as *CUP*.

3. *CUP*, p. 20.

4. Gregor Malantschuk has claimed that *PF* is Kierkegaard's "most abstract" work. "This abstract presentation was required in order to pose the problem as sharply as possible. A more historical-concrete account of this difference between the human and the Christian involves the danger that the boundaries would not be explicitly drawn." See Malantschuk, *Kierkegaard's Thought*, trans. Howard Hong and Edna Hong (Princeton: Princeton University Press, 1971,), p. 245.

5. See the summary of the form and structure of *PF* offered by Niels Thulstrup in his "Commentator's Introduction," *PF*, pp. lxvii–lxxxiv.

6. David Swenson, "Translator's Introduction," *PF*, p. xv.

7. *PF*, p. 137; *CUP*, p. 18.

8. For Kierkegaard's own account of the standpoint of *PF* and *CUP*, see "A First and Last Declaration," attached to the end of *CUP*.

9. This and the next several quotations are from *PF*, pp. 11–18 and 73.

10. As Thulstrup points out, it is important to resist understanding *PF* as though it is written "in a 'world historical' perspective of traditional dogmatics;" instead, it is Kierkegaard's experimental attempt to work through traditional dogmatic expressions in terms of his category of "the moment." Thulstrup, "Commentary," *PF*, pp. 191–92.

11. In large part, one of the chief aims of *PF* seems to be to make the reader "category conscious." The actual categories with which Kierkegaard is operating reflect his wide reading in the history of philosophy, from Plato and Aristotle, to Descartes, Leibniz, Spinoza, and Hegel. See Charles R. Magel, "An Analysis of Kierkegaard's Philosophical Categories," Ph.D. Thesis, University of Minnesota, 1960.

12. *PF*, p. 43. The next four quotations are from pp. 19, 22, 23, and 130.

13. Helpful discussions of Hegel's alternative include Stephen Crites, *In the Twilight of Christendom: Hegel vs. Kierkegaard on Faith and History* (Chambersburg: American Academy of Religion, 1972), esp. chapter 2, and James Yerkes, *The Christology of Hegel* (Missoula: Scholars Press and the American Academy of Religion, 1978), esp. ch. 3.

14. As Kierkegaard makes clear in chapter 2 of *PF*, "The God as Teacher and Saviour: An Essay of the Imagination," pp. 28–45.

15. *PF*, pp. 18–19. The next two quotations are from pp. 18–19.

16. Henry Allison, *Lessing and the Enlightenment* (Ann Arbor: University of Michigan Press, 1966), p. 121.

17 This and the next two quotations are from *CUP*, pp. 25, 26n., and 31.

18. *PF*, p. 118.

19. The following account of the "Interlude" (including quotations) is from *PF*, pp. 89–110, esp. pp. 90–93.

20. See Thulstrup's "Commentary" in *PF*, p. 233.

21. *PF*, p. 101. "Belief" here is the translation of the Danish *Tro*. It is variously translated as "belief" (to denote the apprehension of a historical event in the normal

sense) and as "Faith" (to denote the apprehension of the historical event of the incarnation).

22. Malantschuk, *Kierkegaard's Thought* (p. 255), calls this differentiation process the "central concern" of the "Interlude."

23. This and the following two quotes are from *PF*. pp. 100–104.

24. Hermann Diem, *Dogmatics*, trans. Harold Knight (Philadelphia: Westminster Press, 1959), p. 17. See the parallel discussion in Diem, *Kierkegaard's Dialectic of Existence*, trans. Harold Knight (London: Oliver and Boyd, 1959), pp. 61ff.

25. Diem, *Dogmatics*, p. 17.

26. Such a view would anticipate the theory of reenactment offered by R.G. Collingwood, *The Idea of History* (Oxford: Oxford University Press, 1946).

27. Diem, *Dogmatics*, p. 17.

28. *PF*, p. 23.

29. "[It] is important above all that there be a fixed and unshakeable qualitative difference between *the historical element in Christianity* (the paradox that the eternal came into existence once in time) and *the history of Christianity*. . . . The fact that God came into existence in human form under the Emperor Augustus: that is the historical element in Christianity, the historical in paradoxical composition. It is with this paradox that everyone, in whatever country he may be living, must become contemporary, if he is to become a believing Christian." Kierkegaard, *On Authority and Revelation* ("The Book on Adler"), trans. Walter Lowrie (Princeton: Princeton University Press, 1955), pp. 58–59.

30. For example, *CUP*, pp. 38, 46–47.

31. Diem, *Dogmatics*, p. 17, emphasis added. See also Diem, *Kierkegaard's Dialectic of Existence*, pp. 63–64.

32. *PF*, p. 105.

33. Ibid., p. 106.

34. Arthur Danto, *Analytical Philosophy of History* (Cambridge: Cambridge University Press, 1965), p. 110.

CHAPTER 5

1. This quotation and the next are from *PF*, p. 73 (emphasis added), while the following two quotes are from pp. 130 and 46.

2. *CUP*, pp. 165–66.

3. For helpful discussions of Kierkegaard's employment of the category of paradox, see Malcolm L. Diamond, *Contemporary Philosophy and Religious Thought* (New York: McGraw-Hill, 1974), pp. 156–57, 168–71; R.T. Herbert, *Paradox and Identity* (Ithaca: Cornell University Press, 1979), chs. 3 and 4; and Alastair McKinnon, "Kierkegaard: 'Paradox' and Irrationalism," in *Essays on Kierkegaard*, ed. Jerry H. Gill (Minneapolis: Burgess, 1969), pp. 102–12.

4. Cited by Hermann Diem, *Kierkegaard's Dialectic of Existence*, trans. Harold Knight (London: Oliver and Boyd, 1959), p. 50.

5. This comparison is suggested by Helmut Bintz, *Das Skandalon als Grundlagenproblem der Dogmatik* (Berlin: Verlag Walter de Gruyter, 1969), pp. 73–75.

6. *PF*, ch. 3. The discussion here is taken from pp. 30, 64–77.

7. See also Kierkegaard's own discussion of the standpoint of the Johannes Clima-

cus works in *On Authority and Revelation* ("The Book on Adler"), trans. Walter Lowrie (Princeton: Proinceton University Press, 1955), ch. 2.

8. *PF*, p. 130. The next three quotations are from pp. 76–77, 73, and 76.

9. Ibid., p. 81. For further discussion of this point, see Stephen Crites, *In the Twilight of Christendom: Hegel vs. Kierkegaard on Faith and History* (Chambersburg: American Academy of Religion, 1972), pp. 64–65.

10. *PF*, p. 79. The next two quotations are from pp. 77 and 108.

11. Ibid., p. 108. See Thulstrup's "Commentary" in *PF*, p. 251.

12. Swenson has even capitalized "Faith" when it is meant "in the eminent sense."

13. *PF*, pp. 126–31. "Believes" is not quite the right word, not because Kierkegaard denies an informative content to faith, but because his accent is upon what Crites, *In the Twilight of Christendom* (p. 64), calls "a fundamental transformation of the self." The notion of "believing" is misleading, in other words, if it suggests the assent to "doctrine." As Kierkegaard puts it, "Faith constitutes a sphere all by itself, and every misunderstanding of Christianity may at once be recognized by its transforming it into a doctrine, transferring it to the sphere of the intellectual" (*CUP*, p. 291). At the same time that Kierkegaard wants to stress the existential and subjective "how" of faith, however, he still wants to retain an "object" of faith: "The object of faith is thus God's reality in existence as a particular individual, the fact that God has existed as an individual human being" (*CUP*, p. 290). After all, it is this "object" of faith that keeps Kierkegaard from falling back into the Socratic-idealist mode.

14. Kierkegaard refers to the "eyes of faith" in *PF*, pp. 80, 87, and 128. The following quotations are from *PF*, pp. 115, 124, and 128–32.

15. Kierkegaard's distinction here seems somewhat forced: "The successor believes *by means of* (this expresses the occasional) the testimony of the contemporary, and *in virtue of* the condition he receives from the God" (*PF*, p. 131).

16. *PF*, p. 128. The following quotations are from pp. 105, 130, 129, 125, and 130.

17. *CUP*, p. 89.

18. *PF*, p. 74.

19. Kierkegaard, *Fear and Trembling*, trans. Walter Lowrie (Princeton: Princeton University Press, 1970), esp. pp. 49ff.

CHAPTER 6

1. Ernst Troeltsch, "Über historische und dogmatische Methode in der Theologie," *Gesammelte Schriften*, vol. 2 (Tübingen: J.C.B. Mohr, 1913), pp. 729–53; Troeltsch, "Historiography," in *Encyclopedia of Religion and Ethics*, vol. 6, ed. James Hastings (New York: Charles Scribner's Sons, 1914), pp. 716–23; Van A. Harvey, *The Historian and the Believer* (New York: Macmillan, 1966). See the excellent discussions of Troeltsch and his relation to modern theology by Robert Morgan, "Ernst Troeltsch on Theology and Religion," and "Troeltsch and Christian Theology," both in *Ernst Troeltsch: Writings on Theology and Religion*, ed. Robert Morgan and Michael Pye (Atlanta: John Knox Press, 1977), pp. 1–51, 208–33; and "Ernst Troeltsch and the Dialectical Theology," in *Ernst Troeltsch and the Future of Theology*, ed. John Powell Clayton (Cambridge: Cambridge University Press, 1976), pp. 33–77.

2. Harvey, *The Historian and the Believer*, p. 5.

3. Troeltsch, "Historiography."

4. Morgan, "Troeltsch and Christian Theology," p. 221.

5. Harvey, *The Historian and the Believer*, pp. 14–15.

6. Ibid.

7. Whether practicing historians are as conscious of some of these presuppositional issues as, say, recent analytical philosophers of history is an open question. Also unsettled is the conclusion to be drawn from the answer to the *first* question.

8. Paul Tillich, *Systematic Theology*, vol. 2 (Chicago: University of Chicago Press, 1957), p. 107.

9. Tillich, "Foreword" to Martin Kähler, *The So-Called Historical Jesus and the Historic Biblical Christ*, trans. Carl E. Braaten (Philadelphia: Fortress Press, 1964), p. xii.

10. John Knox, *The Church and the Reality of Christ* (New York: Harper and Row, 1962), p. 16. Cited by Peter Carnley, "The Poverty of Historical Skepticism," *Christ, Faith and History*, ed. S.W. Sykes and J.P. Clayton (Cambridge: Cambridge University Press, 1972), p. 166.

11. Wolfhart Pannenberg, of course, attempts just such a positive correlation. I discuss his effort in chapter 7. A less ambitious attempt at a positive correlation of theology and historical method is offered by Peter C. Hodgson in his book on F.C. Baur, *The Formation of Historical Theology* (New York: Harper and Row, 1966), chapter 6.

12. In his several essays cited above, Robert Morgan attempts to free Troeltsch from certain stereotypes which have been imposed on him by dialectical theologians and others, and which have contributed to the relative neglect of Troeltsch within constructive theology in this century.

13. See, for example, Morgan, "Ernst Troeltsch and the Dialectical Theology," pp. 35ff.

14. In an image worthy of Lessing himself, Kähler spoke of historical criticism as a "never-ending screw" (p. 109 of *The So-Called Historical Jesus and the Historic Biblical Christ*).

15. Herrmann's chief work is *The Communion of the Christian with God*, ed. Robert T. Voelkel (Philadelphia: Fortress Press, 1971).

16. Daniel L. Deegan, "Wilhelm Herrmann: A Reassessment," *Scottish Journal of Theology* 19 (1966): 195.

17. Rudolph Bultmann, "On the Question of Christology," in *Faith and Understanding*, ed. Robert W. Funk and trans. Louise Pettibone Smith (New York: Harper and Row, 1969), pp. 132ff.

18. On Kierkegaard's influence, see Hermann Diem, *Dogmatics*, trans. Harold Knight (Philadelphia: Westminster Press, 1959), esp. pp. 21ff.

19. Karl Barth, *Protestant Thought: From Rousseau to Ritschl*, trans. Biran Cozens (New York: Simon and Schuster, 1959), p. 389. The complete sentence indicates that Barth is laughing at the problems disclosed by Feuerbach, as well as Strauss—an interesting pairing, in light of one of the subplots of the current study, which is that in avoiding the problems raised by Strauss (and historical criticism generally), modern theologians run the risk of falling prey to Feuerbach.

20. Morgan, "Ernst Troeltsch and the Dialectical Theology," p. 66.

21. As I have been suggesting all along in this study, the very possibility of a *sturmfreies Gebiet* for theology is probably dependent upon a Kantian epistemology.

22. It is revealing that this interest in Luther coincides within German academic life with a renewed interest in Kant. The combined influence of Luther and Kant is decisive for the character of Continental theology following World War I. See Morgan, "Troeltsch and Christian Theology," pp. 209ff. Troeltsch's fate in the twentieth

century, incidentally, may be due in part to the fact that he failed to "subscribe to any of the preferred Luthers of the day" (Morgan, "Troeltsch and Christian Theology," p. 210). On the Luther renaissance and its relation to Kant research, see A.O. Dyson, *The Immortality of the Past* (London: SCM Press, LTD, 1974), pp. 59ff. Dyson draws attention to the important monograph by Bruno Bauch, *Luther und Kant* (Berlin: Verlag von Reuther & Reichard, 1904), where Bauch posits a connection between Luther's distinction between dogmatic and intrinsic belief, and Kant's distinction between theoretical and practical reason. A great deal of modern theological controversy—particularly with respect to the subject-object problem—is no doubt a series of variations on these two distinctions, whatever the actual historical connections between Luther and Kant may be.

23. See the discussion of this neo-Reformation theme in Gerhard Ebeling, "The Significance of the Critical Historical Method for Church and Theology in Protestantism," *Word and Faith*, trans. James W. Leitch (Philadelphia: Fortress Press, 1963), esp. pp. 56ff.

24. Bultmann, "On the Question of Christology," p. 132.

25. Harvey, *The Historian and the Believer*, pp. 17–18.

26. Ibid.

27. Morgan, "Ernst Troeltsch and the Dialectical Theology," pp. 58ff. See also Hans W. Frei, "Niebuhr's Theological Background," in *Faith and Ethics*, ed. Paul Ramsey (New York: Harper and Row, 1957),pp. 21ff.

28. "The only way to preserve the unworldly, transcendental character of the divine activity is to regard it not as an interference in worldly happenings, but something accomplished *in* them in such a way that the closed weft of history as it presents itself to objective observation is left undisturbed. To every other eye than the eye of faith the action of God is hidden. Only the 'natural' happening is generally visible and ascertainable. In it is accomplished the hidden act of God." Bultmann, "Bultmann Replies to His Critics," in *Kerygma and Myth*, ed. Hans Werner Bartsch and trans. Reginald H. Fuller (New York: Harper and Row, 1961), p. 197.

29. Even Pannenberg, who emphasizes a positive correlation between faith and historical inquiry, repudiates this approach.

30. Bultmann, "Liberal Theology and the Latest Theological Movement," in *Faith and Understanding*, pp. 45–46.

31. Morgan, "Ernst Troeltsch and the Dialectical Theology," p. 54.

32. In what follows, I am borrowing liberally from Peter Carnley, "The Poverty of Historical Skepticism," esp. pp. 180ff.

33. Troubles which can make the question "How do we know there ever was a past?" an authentic philosophical question.

34. Arthur Danto, *Analytical Philosophy of History* (Cambridge: Cambridge University Press, 1965), pp. 65–66.

35. Carnley, "The Poverty of Historical Skepticism," pp. 180–81.

36. Ibid., p. 185.

37. W.V.O. Quine, "Two Dogmas of Empiricism," in *From a Logical Point of View*, 2d ed. (New York: Harper and Row, 1963), pp. 20–46.

38. Richard Rorty, "Keeping Philosophy Pure," *Yale Review* 65 (1976): 345–46.

39. I have dealt with the relevant philosophical issues in greater detail in "Theology, Historical Knowledge, and the Contingency-Necessity Distinction," *International Journal for Philosophy of Religion* 14 (1983): 87–98.

40. A clear-headed discussion of the theologies of Schubert Ogden and David Tracy within the context of this general issue is offered by William M. Shea, "Revi-

sionist Foundational Theology," *Anglican Theological Review* 57 (1976): 263–79. Correctly, in my view, Shea points out that the approach toward rapprochment with the culture, adopted by both Ogden and Tracy, leaves very much up in the air the question of a sound ecclesiology.

41. The phrase is Thomas Sheehan's in his review of Karl Rahner's *Foundations of Christian Faith: An Introduction to the Idea of Christianity*, in the *New York Review of Books* 29 (February 4, 1982); 14.

42. On the very different forms of mediating theology, see Hans W. Frei, *The Eclipse of Biblical Narrative* (New Haven: Yale University Press, 1974), pp. 124–30, especially the catalogue of names on p. 128.

43. William Nicholls, *Systematic and Philosophical Theology* (Harmondsworth: Penguin Books, 1969), p. 219.

44. I think this applies to debates over the post-Bultmannian "new quest" of the historical Jesus. Posed in terms of whether or not the Christian understanding of existence was available, through existentialist historiography, in the historical Jesus as well as in the kerygma of the early church, the issue *really* turns on what one wishes to do with Bultmann's "act of God" in the cross-resurrection sequence. The issue, in other words, turns on where and how one locates revelation.

45. Bultmann, of course, would always insist that to speak of an "act of God" was not to speak mythologically but analogically. See, for example, *Jesus Christ and Mythology* (New York: Charles Scribner's Sons, 1958), chapter 5.

46. In this country, the point was argued most forcefully by Schubert M. Ogden, *Christ Without Myth* (New York: Harper and Row, 1961). See Bultmann's own revealing review of Ogden, *Journal of Religion* 42 (1962): 225–27. For a discussion that is critical of Ogden's interpretation of Bultmann—where it is suggested that Bultmann's supposed inconsistency is in fact "Ogden's own special, and somewhat private, perception of the issue"—see Thomas C. Oden, "The Alleged Structural Inconsistency in Bultmann," *Journal of Religion* 44 (1964): 193–200.

47. Bultmann, "New Testament and Mythology," in *Kerygma and Myth*, pp. 1–44, esp. pp. 19–33; "Bultmann Replies to His Critics," pp. 201–7; "The Historicity of Man and Faith," in *Existence and Faith*, ed. and trans. Schubert M. Ogden (Cleveland: World, 1960), pp. 92–110.

48. Ogden, *Christ Without Myth*, p. 112. The next quotation is from the same page.

49. Bultmann, "New Testament and Mythology," pp. 29–33; "The Historicity of Man and Faith," pp. 95, 107–10. The technical way of putting the issue is to ask if authentic human existence as an *ontological* possibility can become on *ontic* possibility apart from an act of God.

50. Bultmann, *Jesus Christ and Mythology*, chapter 5.

51. Ibid., p. 43.

52. Jeffrey Stout, *The Flight from Authority* (Notre Dame: University of Notre Dame Press, 1981), p. 147.

53. When I once used the expression "distinctively Christian" in Ogden's presence, he leaned over and said in a stage whisper, "There's no such thing as 'distinctively Christian.'"

54. Bultmann, "Review of Ogden's *Christ Without Myth*," p. 226.

55. Ogden, *Christ Without Myth*, p. 144. The next four quotations are from pp. 124, 140, 143, and 144.

56. Ogden, "On Revelation," in *Our Common History as Christians: Essays in Honor of Albert C. Outler*, ed. John Deschner, Leroy T. Howe, and Klaus Penzel (New York: Oxford University Press, 1975), p. 285.

57. Ogden, "On Revelation," pp. 266–67.
58. Ogden, "On Revelation," pp. 269ff.; Ogden, *Christ Without Myth*, pp. 153ff. It is not entirely clear how Ogden's claim that Jesus is the "decisive" manifestation of the divine love fits together with his claim that authentic existence is possible apart from reference to Jesus. "Decisive" would appear to be a stronger adjective than Ogden either wants or needs.
59. Ogden, "On Revelation," p. 286.
60. This aspect of Ogden's thought finds a clear parallel in the work of David Tracy.
61. See the title essay in Ogden's *The Reality of God* (New York: Harper and Row, 1966), pp. 1–70.
62. Ogden, *Christ Without Myth*, p. 130. Ogden's position has been more thoroughly worked out in his *The Point of Christology* (San Francisco: Harper and Row, 1982), yet the basic structure of his christological position has remained unchanged, as reflected in his reference to his new book as an opportunity "to fill out the christological ouline I projected some two decades ago in *Christ Without Myth*," p. ix.

CHAPTER 7

1. Peter C. Hodgson, *The Formation of Historical Theology* (New York: Harper and Row, 1966), p. 273.
2. Cartesianism in both philosophy and theology has remarkable staying power, in light of the bad things said about it. For a powerful critique from the philosophical side, see Richard Rorty, *Philosophy and the Mirror of Nature* (Princeton: Princeton University Press, 1979) as well as Rorty's more recently published collection of essays, *Consequences of Pragmatism* (Minneapolis: University of Minnesota Press, 1982). Barth's theology—at least from his Anselm book (1931) on—can be viewed as a consistently anti-Cartesian project. For a summary of this unfortunately neglected issue, see Robert E. Cushman, "Barth's Attack Upon Cartesianism and the Future in Theology," *Journal of Religion* 36 (1956): 207–23. In their own very different way, of course, Whiteheadean theologians are attempting to undo the conceptual damage effected by Cartesianism.
3. With respect to Kierkegaard, this point is brought out with consistency and rigor by Mark Taylor in *Kierkegaard's Pseudonymous Authorship: A Study of Time and the Self* (Princeton: Princeton University Press, 1975). See as well Taylor's more recent work, *Journeys to Selfhood: Hegel and Kierkegaard* (Berkeley: University of California Press, 1980).
4. For translations of early discussions of these issues, see James M. Robinson (ed.), *The Beginnings of Dialectical Theology*, trans. Keith R. Crim, Louis De Grazia (Richmond: John Knox Press, 1968).
5. For example, Van A. Harvey, *The Historian and the Believer* (New York: Macmillan, 1966), chapter 5.
6. The transition point was Barth's *Anselm: Fides Quaerens Intellectum*, trans. I.W. Robertson (New York: World, 1960). The most useful discussion of Barth's transition remains Hans W. Frei, "Niebuhr's Theological Background," in *Faith and Ethics*, ed. Paul Ramsey (New York: Harper and Row, 1957), pp. 40–53.
7. Barth, *Fragments Grave and Gay* (London: Fontana, 1971), p. 99. Cited by

Philip C. Almond, "Karl Barth and Anthropocentric Theology," *Scottish Journal of Theology* 31 (1978): 441–42.

8. Looking back on the early 1920s, Barth would later say of his relation with Bultmann: "I thought I understood him and perhaps he thought he understood me. Certainly we sometimes said the same kind of thing." Barth's emerging suspicions about his colleague were confirmed during a visit between the two in Göttingen, in 1925. According to Barth, "We sat down one Saturday in a small village outside Göttingen to have coffee and buns," and Bultmann "read aloud for hours from lectures by Martin Heidegger which he had heard and written down in Marburg. The purpose of the exercise was that we should attempt to understand the gospel witnessed to by the New Testament, like all matters of the spirit, by means of this 'existentialist' approach." Quoted in Eberhard Busch, *Karl Barth: His Life from Letters and Autobiographical Texts*, trans. John Bowden (Philadelphia: Fortress Press, 1976), pp. 136, 161.

9. In his Transcendental Deduction in the *Critique of Pure Reason*, Kant establishes a crucial link between the conditions of self-consciousness and the conditions of objective knowledge: by getting to the former (through his notion of the "unity of apperception"), Kant thinks he has gotten to the latter as well. Beginning almost immediately with Fichte, philosophers have, ever since, been trying to figure out what to do or say about this Kantian move. *Critique of Pure Reason*, trans. Norman Kemp-Smith (New York: St. Martin's Press, 1965), B137–39, pp. 156–57.

10. Hermann Diem, *Dogmatics*, trans. Harold Knight (Philadelphia: Westminster Press, 1959), pp. 35ff.; A.O. Dyson, *The Immortality of the Past* (London: SCM Press, LTD, 1974), p. 61.

11. H. Iwand, "Wider den Missbrauch des 'pro me' als methodisches Prinzip in der Theologie," *Theologische Literaturzeitung* 79 (1954); 453–58.

12. Dyson, *The Immortality of the Past*, p. 62. This general problem is discussed in detail, with particular attention to its Cartesian aspects, by Helmut Thielicke, *The Evangelical Faith*, vol. 1, trans. Geoffrey W. Bromiley (Grand Rapids: William B. Eerdmanns, 1974), part 1.

13. Alasdair MacIntyre, "The Fate of Theism," in MacIntyre and Paul Ricoeur, *The Religious Significance of Atheism* (New York and London: Columbia University Press, 1969), p. 24.

14. MacIntyre, "God and the Theologians," *Against the Self-Images of the Age* (Notre Dame: University of Notre Dame Press, 1978), p. 18.

15. This is the general point of both of the MacIntyre works just cited, as well as of his concluding remarks in "Is Understanding Religion Compatible with Believing?" in *Rationality*, ed. Bryan R. Wilson (New York: Harper and Row, 1970), pp. 74–77.

16. MacIntyre suggests that theologians such as Bultmann and Tillich attempt restatements of Christian theism that both "distinguish the theistic kernel from the theistic husk" and are "intelligible to contemporary educated, secular-minded men." MacIntyre maintains that "these aims are essentially incompatible with each other; that any presentation of theism which is able to secure a hearing from a secular audience has undergone a transformation that has evacuated it entirely of its theistic content. Conversely, any presentation which retains such theistic content will be unable to secure the place in contemporary culture which those theologians desire for it." "The Fate of Theism," p. 26.

17. W. Pannenberg, "Insight and Faith," *Basic Questions in Theology*, vol. 2, trans. George H. Kehm (Philadelphia: Fortress Press, 1971), pp. 30–33.

18. Ibid., p. 28.

19. Ibid., pp. 34, 36.

20. Ibid., p. 32. The motivation behind Pannenberg's criticism of modern Protestant views of history is succinctly expressed in the following passage: "All theological questions and answers are meaningful only within the framework of the history which God has with humanity and through humanity with his whole creation—the history moving toward a future still hidden from the world but already revealed in Jesus Christ. This presupposition of Christian theology must be defended today within theology itself on two sides: on the one side, against Bultmann and Gogarten's existential theology which dissolves history into the historicity of existence; on the other side, against the thesis, developed by Martin Kähler in the tradition of redemptive history, that the real content of faith is suprahistorical." "Redemptive Event and History," *Basic Questions in Theology*, vol. 1 (1970), p. 15.

21. Pannenberg, "Redemptive Event and History," p. 56.

22. Ibid., pp. 54–56; Pannenberg, *Jesus: God and Man*, trans. Lewis L. Wilkins and Duane Priebe (Philadelphia: Westmister Press, 1968), p. 27. Herrmann himself, of course, is subject to the same charge that he levels against Kähler.

23. Pannenberg, *Jesus: Man and God*, p. 109.

24. Pannenberg, "The Revelation of God in Jesus of Nazareth," in *New Frontiers in Theology*, ed. James M. Robinson and John B. Cobb, Jr. (New York: Harper and Row, 1967), p. 128. The "event" that Pannenberg has especially in mind is the resurrection of Jesus. However, see my criticism of the misleading character of his historical-critical approach to the resurrection, in "Pannenberg on the Resurrection and Historical Method," *Scottish Journal of Theology* 33 (1980): 345–59.

25. Pannenberg, "Insight and Faith," p. 33.

26. Pannenberg's most forceful statement of this position is his *Theology and the Philosophy of Science*, trans. Francis McDonagh (Philadelphia: Westminster Press, 1976).

27. In an odd sort of way, Pannenberg's demand that faith really *claim* something that would make a difference matches the position of Antony Flew, who rejects religious language as meaningless on the grounds that there is "no conceivable event or series of events the occurrence of which would be admitted by sophisticated religious people to be a sufficient reason for conceding 'There wasn't a God after all' or 'God does not really love us then.' " "Theology and Falsification," in *New Essays in Philosophical Theology*, ed. Antony Flew and Alasdair MacIntyre (London: SCM Press, 1955), p. 98. It is ironic that Pannenberg should be injecting a parallel issue into Continental theological discussions just as the verificationist-falsificationist debate has run its course in the English-speaking world.

28. In addition to Lessing's interest in the Moravians, there were of course the biographical circumstances linking both Kant and Schleiermacher to the pietism of their time.

29. Pannenberg maintains that the argument "that faith loses its independence by being bound to the results of historical research and thus subjected to the authority of science, exhibits a peculiarly neo-Protestant (or, if you like, pietistic) character from start to finish." "Redemptive Event and History," p. 56.

30. Pannenberg, "Kerygma and History," *Basic Questions*, vol. 1, p. 86.

31. Pannenberg, "Redemptive Event and History," pp. 54ff.

32. Pannenberg, *Jesus: Man and God*, pp. 88–106.

33. Pannenberg, "Redemptive Event and History," p. 56.

34. Ibid.

35. This insistence on a nondualistic view of history permeates Pannenberg's three key essays on the topic: "Redemptive Event and History"; "Kerygma and History"; and "Hermeneutic and Universal History," *Basic Questions*, vol. 1, pp. 96–136.

36. Pannenberg, "The Revelation of God in Jesus of Nazareth," pp. 126–27.

37. The programmatic statement of this position is the early (1961) work by Pannenberg and several colleagues, *Revelation as History*, ed. W. Pannenberg (New York: Macmillan, 1968).

38. See, for example, Pannenberg, *Jesus: God and Man*, pp. 181–83.

39. Pannenberg, *Revelation as History*, pp. 133ff.

40. Thus, Pannenberg's interest in the idea of *Überlieferungsgeschichte* ("history of the transmission of traditions") and his interest in H.G. Gadamer's image of *Horizontverschmelzung* ("fusion of horizons") when dealing with the problem of hermeneutics. See, for example, Pannenberg, "Hermeneutic and Universal History," esp. pp. 115ff.

41. This contextualism, together with Pannenberg's anti-Kantian epistemology, constitute two of the several points of contact between him and American and British process theologians.

42. Pannenberg, "Appearance as the Arrival of the Future," *Journal of the American Academy of Religion* 35 (1967): 111ff.

43. Pannenberg, *Revelation as History*, p. 131.

44. Pannenberg, *Jesus: God and Man*, pp. 53ff.

Bibliography

Allison, Henry. *Lessing and the Enlightenment.* Ann Arbor: University of Michigan Press, 1966.

Almond, Philip C. "Karl Barth and Anthropocentric Theology," *Scottish Journal of Theology* 31 (1978).

Baillie, John. *The Idea of Revelation in Recent Thought.* New York: Harper and Row, 1956.

Barth, Karl. *Anselm: Fides Quaerens Intellectum.* Trans. I.W. Robertson. New York: World, 1960.

———. *Church Dogmatics.* Vols. 1–4. Trans. T.F. Torrance et al. Edinburgh: T. and T. Clark LTD, 1936–1958.

———. *Protestant Thought: From Rousseau to Ritschl.* Trans. Brian Cozens. New York: Simon and Schuster, 1959.

———. "Rudolph Bultmann: An Attempt to Understand Him." In Vol. 2 of *Kerygma and Myth,* ed. Hans Werner Bartsch and trans. Reginald H. Fuller. London: SPCK, 1962.

Bauch, Bruno. *Luther und Kant.* Berlin: Verlag von Reuther and Reichard, 1904.

Bintz, Helmut. *Das Skandalon als Grundlagenproblem der Dogmatik.* Berlin: Verlag Walter de Gruyter, 1969.

Bultmann, Rudolph. *Existence and Faith.* Ed. and trans. Schubert M. Ogden. Cleveland: World Publishing, 1960.

———. *Faith and Understanding.* Trans. Louise Pettibone Smith. New York: Harper and Row, 1969.

———. *Jesus Christ and Mythology.* New York: Charles Scribner's Sons, 1958.

———. *Kerygma and Myth.* Ed. Hans Werner Bartsch and trans. Reginald H. Fuller. New York: Harper and Row, 1961.

———. "The Primitive Christian Kerygma and the Historical Jesus." In *The Historical Jesus and the Kerygmatic Christ,* ed. Carl E. Braaten and Roy Harrisville. Nashville: Abingdon Press, 1964.

———. "Review of *Christ Without Myth.*" *Journal of Religion* 42 (1962).

Busch, Eberhard. *Karl Barth: His Life From Letters and Autobiographical Texts.* Trans. John Bowden. Philadelphia: Fortress Press, 1976.

Campbell, Richard. "Lessing's Problem and Kierkegaard's Answer." *Scottish Journal of Theology* 19 (1966).

Carnley, Peter. "The Poverty of Historical Skepticism." In *Christ, Faith, and History,* ed. S.W. Sykes and J.P. Clayton. Cambridge: Cambridge University Press, 1972.

Cassirer, Ernst. *The Philosophy of the Enlightenment.* Trans. Fritz C.A. Koelln and James P. Pettegrove. Princeton: Princeton University Press, 1951.

Crites, Stephen. "The Gospel According to Hegel." *Journal of Religion* 46 (1966).

————. *In the Twilight of Christendom: Hegel Vs. Kierkegaard on Faith and History*. Chambersburg, Pa.: American Academy of Religion, 1971.

Cushman, Robert. "Barth's Attack upon Cartesianism and the Future in Theology." *Journal of Religion* 36 (1956).

Deegan, Daniel L. "Martin Kähler: Kerygma and Gospel History." *Scottish Journal of Theology* 16 (1963).

————. "Wilhelm Herrmann: A Reassessment." *Scottish Journal of Theology* 19 (1966).

Despland, Michel. *Kant on History and Religion*. Montreal and London: McGill-Queen's University Press, 1973.

Diamond, Malcolm. *Contemporary Philosophy and Religious Thought*. New York: McGraw-Hill, 1974.

Diem, Hermann. *Dogmatics*. Trans. Harold Knight. Philadelphia: Westminster Press, 1959.

————. *Kierkegaard's Dialectic of Existence*. Trans. Harold Knight. London: Oliver and Boyd, 1959.

Dyson, A.O. *The Immortality of the Past*. London: SCM Press, LTD, 1974.

Ebeling, Gerhard. *Word and Faith*. Trans. James W. Leitch. Philadelphia: Fortress Press, 1963.

Frei, Hans W. *The Eclipse of Biblical Narrative*. New Haven: Yale University Press, 1974.

————. "Niebuhr's Theological Background." In *Faith and Ethics*, ed. Paul Ramsey. New York: Harper and Row, 1957.

Gill, Jerry H., ed. *Essays on Kierkegaard*. Minneapolis: Burgess, 1969.

Hardwick, Charley D. *Faith and Objectivity: Fritz Buri and the Hermeneutical Foundations of a Radical Theology*. The Hague: Martinus Nijhoff, 1972.

Harvey, Van A. "The Alienated Theologian." In *The Future of Philosophical Theology*, ed. Robert A. Evans. Philadelphia: Westminster Press, 1971.

————. *The Historian and the Believer*. New York: Macmillan, 1966.

————. "The Pathos of Liberal Theology." *Journal of Religion* 56 (1976).

Helm, Paul. *The Varieties of Belief*. London: Allen and Unwin, LTD, 1973.

Herbert, R.T. *Paradox and Identity*. Ithaca: Cornell University Press, 1979.

Herrmann, Wilhelm. *The Communion of the Christian With God*. Trans. Robert T. Voelkel. Philadelphia: Fortress Press, 1971.

Hodgson, Peter C. *The Formation of Historical Theology*. New York: Harper and Row, 1966.

Iwand, H. "Wider den Missbrauch des 'pro me' als methodisches Prinzip in der Theologie." *Theologie Literaturzeitung* 79 (1954).

Kähler, Martin. *The So-Called Historical Jesus and the Historic Biblical Christ*. Ed. and trans. Carl E. Braaten. Philadelphia: Fortress Press, 1964.

Kamlah, Wilhelm. *Christentum und Selbstbehauptung*. Frankfurt: Verlag Klostermann, 1940.

Kant, Immanuel. *Kant on History*. Ed. and trans. Lewis White Beck. New York: Bobbs-Merrill, 1963.

————. *Religion Within the Limits of Reason Alone*. Trans. Theodore M. Greene and Hoyt H. Hudson. New York: Harper and Row, 1960.

Keck, Leander. "Editor's Introduction" in David Friedrich Strauss, *The Christ of Faith and the Jesus of History*, ed. Leander Keck. Philadelphia: Fortress Press, 1977.

Kierkegaard, S. *Concluding Unscientific Postscript*. Trans. David W. Swenson and Walter Lowrie. Princeton: Princeton University Press, 1968.

———. *On Authority and Revelation* ("The Book on Adler"). Trans. Walter Lowrie. Princeton: Princeton University Press, 1955.

———. *Philosophical Fragments*. Trans. David W. Swenson and Howard Hong. Princeton: Princeton University Press, 1962.

Lessing, G.E. "Die Erziehung des Menschengeschlechts"; "Das Testament Johannis"; and "Über den Beweis des Geistes und der Kraft." In Vol. 8 of *Gesammelte Werke*, ed. Paul Rilla. Berlin: Aufbau-Verlag, 1956.

———. *Lessing's Theological Writings*. Ed. and trans. Henry Chadwick. Stanford: Stanford University Press, 1956.

———. *Nathan der Weise*. Ed. Peter Demetz. Frankfurt/M and Berlin: Verlag Ullstein, 1966.

Lukács, Georg. *The Young Hegel: Studies in the Relations Between Dialectics and Economics*. Trans. Rodney Livingtone. Cambridge: MIT Press, 1976.

MacIntyre, Alasdair. *Against the Self-Images of the Age*. Notre Dame, Ind.: University of Notre Dame Press, 1978.

———. "Is Understanding Religion Compatible with Believing?" In *Rationality*, ed. Bryan R. Wilson. New York: Harper and Row, 1971.

MacIntyre, Alasdair, and Paul Ricoeur. *The Religious Significance of Atheism*. New York and London: Columbia University Press, 1969.

Malantschuk, George. *Kierkegaard's Thought*. Trans. Howard Hong and Edna Hong. Princeton: Princeton University Press, 1971.

Michalson, G.E., Jr. *The Historical Dimensions of a Rational Faith: The Role of History in Kant's Religious Thought*. Washington, D.C.: University Press of America, 1977.

———. "Lessing, Kierkegaard, and the 'Ugly Ditch': A Reexamination." *Journal of Religion* 59 (1979).

———. "Pannenberg on the Resurrection and Historical Method." *Scottish Journal of Theology* 33 (1980).

———. "Theology, Historical Knowledge, and the Contingency-Necessity Distinction." *International Journal for Philosophy of Religion* 14 (1983).

Morgan, Robert. "Ernst Troeltsch and the Dialectical Theology." In *Ernst Troeltsch and the Future of Theology*, ed. John Powell Clayton. Cambridge: Cambridge University Press, 1976.

———. "Ernst Troeltsch on Theology and Religion" and "Troeltsch and Christian Theology." In *Ernst Troeltsch: Writings on Theology and Religion*, ed. R. Morgan and Michael Pye. Atlanta: John Knox Press, 1977.

Nichol, Iain G. "Facts and Meanings." *Religious Studies* 12 (1976).

Nicholls, William. *Systematic and Philosophical Theology*. Harmondsworth: Penguin, 1969.

Oden, Thomas C. "The Alleged Structural Inconsistency in Bultmann." *Journal of Religion* 44 (1964).

Ogden, Schubert M. *Christ Without Myth*. New York: Harper and Row, 1961.

———. "On Revelation." In *Our Common History as Christians: Essays in Honor of Albert Outler*, ed. John Deschner, Leroy T. Howe, and Klaus Penzel. New York: Oxford University Press, 1975.

———. *The Point of Christology*. San Francisco: Harper and Row, 1982.

———. *The Reality of God*. New York: Harper and Row, 1966.

Pailin, David. "Lessing's Ditch Revisited: The Problem of Faith and History." In *Theology and Change: Essays in Memory of Alan Richardson*, ed. R.H. Preston. London: SCM Press, LTD, 1975.

Pannenberg, Wolfhart. "Appearance as the Arrival of the Future." *Journal of the American Academy of Religion* 35 (1967).

———. *Basic Questions in Theology.* Vols. 1–2. Trans. George H. Kehm. Philadelphia: Fortress Press, 1970; 1971.

———. *Jesus: God and Man.* Trans. Lewis L. Wilkens and Duane Priebe. Philadelphia: Westminster Press, 1968.

———. *Theology and the Philosophy of Science.* Trans. Francis McDonagh. Philadelphia: Westminster Press, 1976.

———, ed. *Revelation as History.* New York: Macmillan, 1968.

Penzel, Klaus. "Church History in Context: The Case of Philip Schaff." In *Our Common History as Christians: Essays in Honor of Albert C. Outler,* ed. John Deschner, Leroy T. Howe, and Klaus Penzel. New York: Oxford University Press, 1975.

Rahner, Karl. *Foundations of the Christian Faith: An Introduction to the Idea of Christianity.* Trans. W.V. Dych. New York: Seabury Press, 1978.

Reardon, Bernard M.G. *Hegel's Philosophy of Religion.* New York: Barnes and Noble, 1977.

Robinson, James M., ed. *The Beginnings of Dialectical Theology.* Trans. Keith R. Crim and Louis De Grazia. Richmond, Vir.: John Knox Press, 1968.

———. *Kerygma und Historischer Jesus.* 2d ed. Zürich: Zwingli Verlag, 1967.

———. *A New Quest of the Historical Jesus.* London: SCM Press, LTD, 1959.

———. "The Recent Debate on the 'New Quest.'" *Journal of Bible and Religion* 30 (1962).

Robinson, James M., and John B. Cobb, Jr., eds. *New Frontiers in Theology.* Vol. 3, *Theology as History.* New York: Harper and Row, 1967.

Rorty, Richard. *Philosophy and the Mirror of Nature.* Princeton: Princeton University Press, 1979.

Ross, J. Robert. "Historical Knowledge as Basis for Faith." *Zygon* 13 (1978).

Schilson, A. *Geschichte im Horizont der Vorsehung: G.E. Lessings Beitrag zur Einer Theologie Der Geschichte.* Mainz: Mattias-Grünewald Verlag, 1974.

Schmitz, Kenneth L. "The Conceptualization Of Religious Mystery: An Essay on Hegel's Philosophy of Religion." In *The Legacy of Hegel,* ed. J.J. O'Malley, K.W. Algozin, H.P. Kainz, and L.C. Rice. The Hague: Martinus Nijhoff, 1973.

Schweitzer, Albert. *Quest of the Historical Jesus.* New York: Macmillan, 1956.

Shea, William M. "Revisionist Foundational Theology." *Anglican Theological Review* 57 (1976).

Stout, Jeffrey. *The Flight From Authority.* Notre Dame: University of Notre Dame Press, 1981.

Swinburne, Richard. *The Concept of Miracle.* London: Macmillan, 1970.

Taylor, Mark. *Journeys to Selfhood: Hegel and Kierkegaard.* Berkeley: University of California Press, 1980.

———. *Kierkegaard's Pseudonymous Authorship: A Study of Time and the Self.* Princeton: Princeton University Press, 1975.

Thielicke, Helmut. *The Evangelical Faith.* Vol. 1. Ed. and trans. Geoffrey Bromiley. Grand Rapids: William B. Eerdmans, 1974.

———. *Offenbarung, Vernunft, und Existenz: Studien zur Religionsphilosophie Lessings.* 4th ed. Gütersloh: Carl Bertelsmann Verlag, 1957.

Thornton, J.C. "Religious Belief and 'Reductionism.'" *Sophia* 5 (1966).

Tillich, Paul. *Systematic Theology.* Vol. 2. Chicago: University of Chicago Press, 1957.

Tracy, David. *Blessed Rage for Order.* New York: Seabury Press, 1975.

Traub, Friedrich. "Geschichtswahrheiten und Vernunftswahrheiten bei Lessing." *Zeitschrift für Theologie und Kirche* 28 (1920).

Troeltsch, Ernst. "Historiography," Vol. 6 of *Encyclopedia of Religion and Ethics*, ed. James Hastings. New York: Charles Scribner's Sons, 1914.

———. "Über historische und dogmatische Methode in der Theologie." *Gesammelte Schriften*. Vol. 2. Tübingen: J.C.B. Mohr, 1913.

Welch, Claude. *Protestant Thought in the Nineteenth Century*. New Haven: Yale University Press, 1972.

Wessel, Leonard. *G.E. Lessing's Theology: A Reinterpretation*. The Hague and Paris: Mouton, 1977.

Wittgenstein, Ludwig. *Philosophical Investigations*. 3rd ed., trans. G.E.M. Anscombe. New York: Macmillan, 1958.

Yerkes, James. *The Christology of Hegel*. Missoula, Mont.: Scholars Press and the American Academy of Religion, 1978.

Index

56, 63, 99–100, 124–26; Pannenberg's
criticism of, 124–27

Eschatology, 14, 110, 115
Evidence: and Kierkegaard, 64, 91; and
Lessing, 8–9, 15, 25; and modern theology, 52–53, 94
Existential ditch, 8, 14–20, 40, 48, 63, 64
Existentialism: and Barth, 119, 145 n. 8;
and Bultmann, 108–15, 119, 143 n. 44,
145 n. 8; and Ogden, 110–15; Pannenberg's criticism of, 122, 124, 146 n. 20;
and theological method, 6, 18, 54,
118–19

Faith. *See* Faith and historical knowledge; Faith and reason; Faith and subjectivity
Faith and historical knowledge: and
Bultmann, 4–7, 18, 97–98, 100, 109,
118; and christology, 35, 55, 96; and
Herrmann, 4–5, 96–97; and Kähler,
4–5, 96, 122; and Kant, 53; and Kierkegaard, 2, 4, 18, 62–63, 71–73, 74,
80, 81, 89, 91–92, 100, 117, 122–23;
and Lessing, 2, 4, 24–27, 37, 39–40,
53, 91–92, 122–23; and Ogden, 110–
15; and Pannenberg, 121–28; as problem for modern theology, 2, 18, 51,
53–55, 91–92, 94–100, 117–19, 122–
24; and Tillich, 95–96; and Troeltsch,
94–100
Faith and reason, 39, 61, 64, 70, 84,
106–15, 121–22
Faith and subjectivity: and Barth, 119–
20; and Bultmann, 109–10; and Cartesianism, 57–58, 117; and Kant, 5, 55–
56, 117; and Kierkegaard, 5, 63, 90–
92, 117; and Lessing, 53–59; and Pannenberg, 121–28; as problem for modern theology, 19, 35, 53–59, 117–28
Feuerbach, Ludwig, 118, 119, 141 n. 19
Fichte, Johann Gottlieb, 145 n. 9
Flew, Antony, 146 n. 27
Frei, Hans W., 3

Gadamer, Hans-Georg, 147 n. 40
Gellner, Ernest, 57
Goeze, Johann Melchior, 15, 136 n. 6

Gogarten, Friedrich, 54, 97, 118, 119,
146 n. 20

Harvey, Van A., 6, 94, 98–99
Hegel, Georg Wilhelm Friedrich, 3, 16,
35, 44, 48, 52, 137 n. 24; and history,
30; and philosophical necessity, 30,
34; relation to Kierkegaard, 30, 61, 66,
67, 69, 83; relation to Pannenberg, 126
Heidegger, Martin, 108, 109, 115, 124,
145 n. 8
Hermeneutics, 18, 33, 39, 57–58, 93,
108–11, 118–19, 147 n. 40
Herrmann, Wilhelm, 4, 5, 54, 96–97,
120, 122, 123, 131 n. 8, 146 n. 22
Historical events, 7, 33, 36, 53, 58, 99,
118; and Bultmann, 110–15; and Kierkegaard, 12, 62, 69, 71, 73, 74, 75–80,
86; and Lessing, 19, 25, 29, 31–32, 37–
39, 42–43, 45; and Ogden, 110–15;
and Pannenberg, 122, 126–27; and
universal truths, 105–15
Historical knowledge: and Kierkegaard,
2, 9–10, 12–13, 21, 65, 71–73, 74–80,
82, 85, 88–89, 91–92; and Lessing, 2,
9–10, 13, 23–27, 29, 30–31, 37, 42,
53; and modern theology, 4–5, 46–47,
53–54, 94–105; and Pannenberg,
122–28; philosophical criticism of,
101–3; relation to contingency-necessity distinction, 103–4; relation to
dogmatic claims, 42–44; relation to
philosophical necessity, 33; and Tillich, 95–96; and Troeltsch, 94–99,
101–5. *See also* Faith and historical
knowledge; Temporal ditch
History. *See* Historical events; Historical
knowledge
Hume, David, 26, 77, 94

Jesus: and historical judgments, 2, 3, 4,
6, 12–13, 23, 29, 53, 55, 64, 93, 95,
124, 126; relation to modern believer,
14, 23; relation to religious truth, 12–
13, 18–19, 24, 36, 43, 45, 65, 68, 96,
106–7, 110–11, 113–15, 126–27

Kähler, Martin, 4, 5, 96–97, 98, 122,
124, 146 n. 20, 146 n. 22
Kamlah, Wilhelm, 18